TEXTS FOR ENGLISH AND AMERICAN STUDIES
edited by
Peter Freese

3

AMERICA, the Melting Pot

Fact and Fiction

edited and annotated
by
Peter Bischoff

STUDENTS' BOOK

Ferdinand Schöningh – Paderborn

Dr. Peter Bischoff, M.A., is *Akademischer Oberrat* in the *Englisches Seminar,*
Westfälische Wilhelms-Universität Münster.

Detailed analyses of the texts in
this Reader, didactic reflections,
and methodological instructions
can be found in the accompanying
TEACHERS' BOOK,
Schöninghbuch 41006

München · Wien · Zürich
Printed in Germany
Herstellung: Ferdinand Schöningh, Paderborn
ISBN 3-506-41005-9

Contents

Titles with an * are provided by the editor.

Abbreviations

AE = American English	derog. = derogatory	pl.n. = plural noun
arch. = archaic	e.g. = for example	p.p. = past participle
adj. = adjective	esp. = especially	poet. = poetically
adv. = adverb	fig. = figuratively	pred.adj. = predicative adjective
attrib. = attributive (ly)	interj. = interjection	prep. = preposition
BE = British English	l(l). = line(s)	s.b. = somebody
cf. = compare	n. = noun	sl. = slang
coll. = colloquial	orig. = originally	spec. = specifically
conj. = conjunction	o.s. = oneself	s.th. = something
	p(p). = page(s)	usu. = usually
	part.adj. = participial adjective	v. = verb

Introduction

The United States is a nation of immigrants. With the exception of the American Indian, all Americans have either come to America from a foreign land or are descendants of immigrants.

The Melting Pot myth was formulated as early as 1782 by Crèvecœur: "Here individuals of all nations are melted into a new race of men." Even in the face of evidence to the contrary, a number of German school readers still cling to the Melting Pot myth as if to propagate a special way of interpreting American history: "The vast majority of immigrants, of whatever origin, tongue, or faith, quickly became good Americans, and showed that they were ready and able to fit into the American way of life."

The present reader aims at putting matters into the right perspective. The texts in this anthology not only trace the development of the Melting Pot myth, but also expose it as a fallacy in the light of historical, social, and literary facts.

Millions of immigrants have crossed the Atlantic and the Pacific to escape poverty, political oppression, religious persecution, or simply to seek adventure, and to find opportunity and prosperity in a land where many thought the streets were paved with gold. This anthology introduces the student to different people's motives for emigration, their hardships in reaching their destination, their difficulties in making a living in America and grappling with a new environment and a new way of life. An effort has been made to give as representative a picture of these things as is possible in the format of such a book. In these texts of various genres the Melting Pot ideology is contrasted with such concepts as "immigration restriction," "a nation of nations," "cultural pluralism" and "ethnicity."

A man in a Chinese restaurant asked for the special of the day.
"Pizza."
"What? Pizza in a Chinese restaurant?"
"Of course. After all, this is a Jewish neighborhood."

Pasquale had to answer the following question at his naturalization examination:
"What's the name of the capital of the United States?"
"Washington."
"And what's the name of our president?"
"McKinley."
"Could you be president of the United States?"
"No."
"Why not?"
"Excusa me, Your Honor, I no hava da time, I gotta sella peanuts all da day."

On Easter Sunday the Irish owner of a drugstore put a sign in his window:
CHRIST HAS RISEN.
The next day his Jewish neighbor put an even larger sign in his window:
BUT COHEN'S PRICES REMAIN THE SAME.

A policeman was walking his beat one night in New York's Central Park. On a wide lawn he found fifty sleeping Puerto Rican men, women, and children. He woke one of the men up.
"What's your name?"
"Esteban Garcia."
"What are all of you people doing here?"
"Our room is being repainted."

Mrs. Teitelbaum said to Mrs. Weizenkorn:
"Did you hear that the bishops in Rome are talking again about Church reform?"
"What are they talking about?"
"That it wasn't the Jews who nailed Jesus on the cross."
"Who then?"
"Don't know exactly. But I believe they suspect the Puerto Ricans."

You don't have to be Jewish

to love Levy's

real Jewish Rye

A NATION

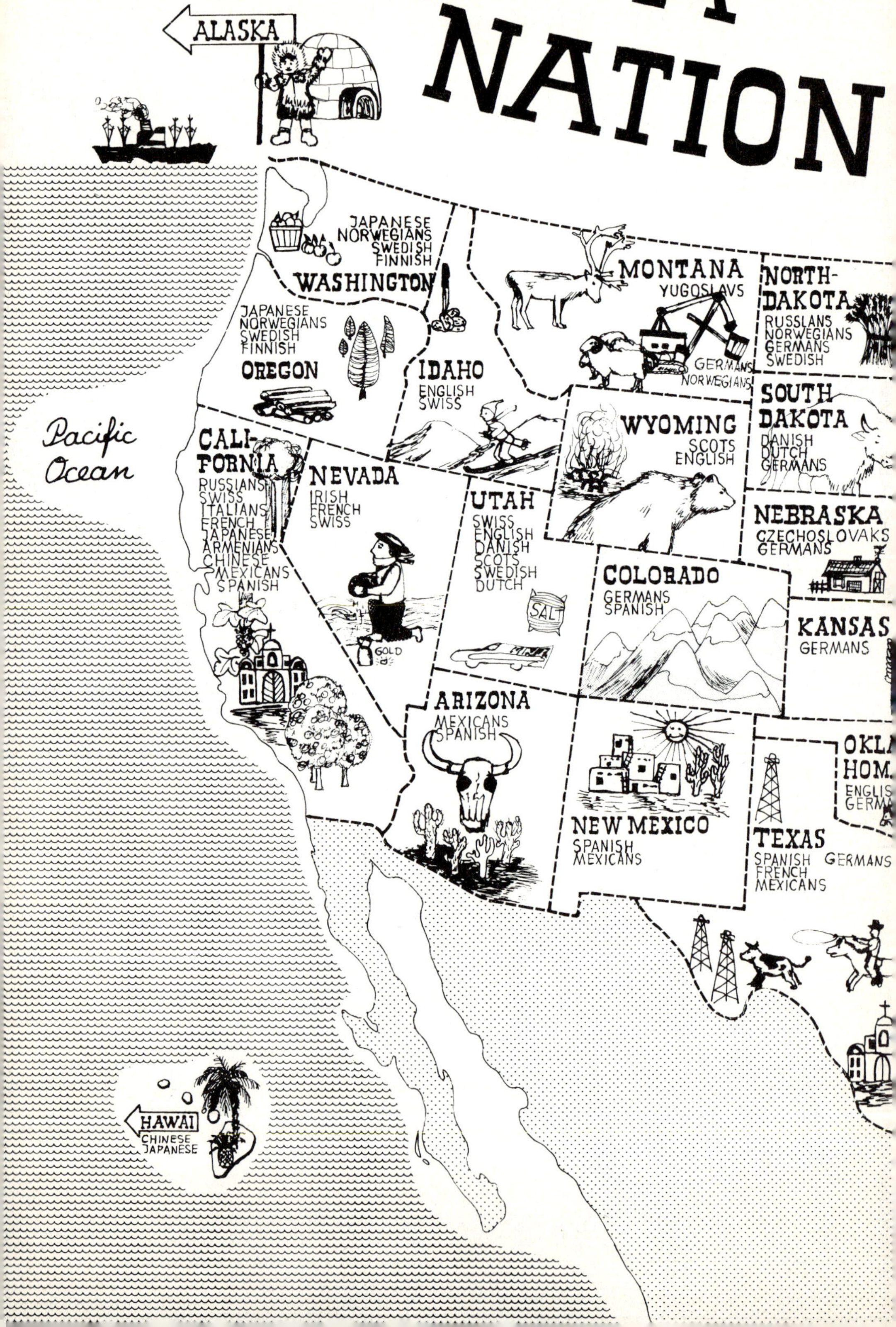
ALASKA
Pacific Ocean
WASHINGTON
JAPANESE
NORWEGIANS
SWEDISH
FINNISH
OREGON
JAPANESE
NORWEGIANS
SWEDISH
FINNISH
CALIFORNIA
RUSSIANS
SWISS
ITALIANS
FRENCH
JAPANESE
ARMENIANS
CHINESE
MEXICANS
SPANISH
NEVADA
IRISH
FRENCH
SWISS
GOLD
IDAHO
ENGLISH
SWISS
MONTANA
YUGOSLAVS
GERMANS
NORWEGIANS
WYOMING
SCOTS
ENGLISH
UTAH
SWISS
ENGLISH
DANISH
SCOTS
SWEDISH
DUTCH
SALT
COLORADO
GERMANS
SPANISH
ARIZONA
MEXICANS
SPANISH
NEW MEXICO
SPANISH
MEXICANS
NORTH-DAKOTA
RUSSIANS
NORWEGIANS
GERMANS
SWEDISH
SOUTH DAKOTA
DANISH
DUTCH
GERMANS
NEBRASKA
CZECHOSLOVAKS
GERMANS
KANSAS
GERMANS
OKLA HOM.
ENGLIS
GERM
TEXAS
SPANISH
FRENCH
MEXICANS
GERMANS
HAWAI
CHINESE
JAPANESE

OF IMMIGRANTS

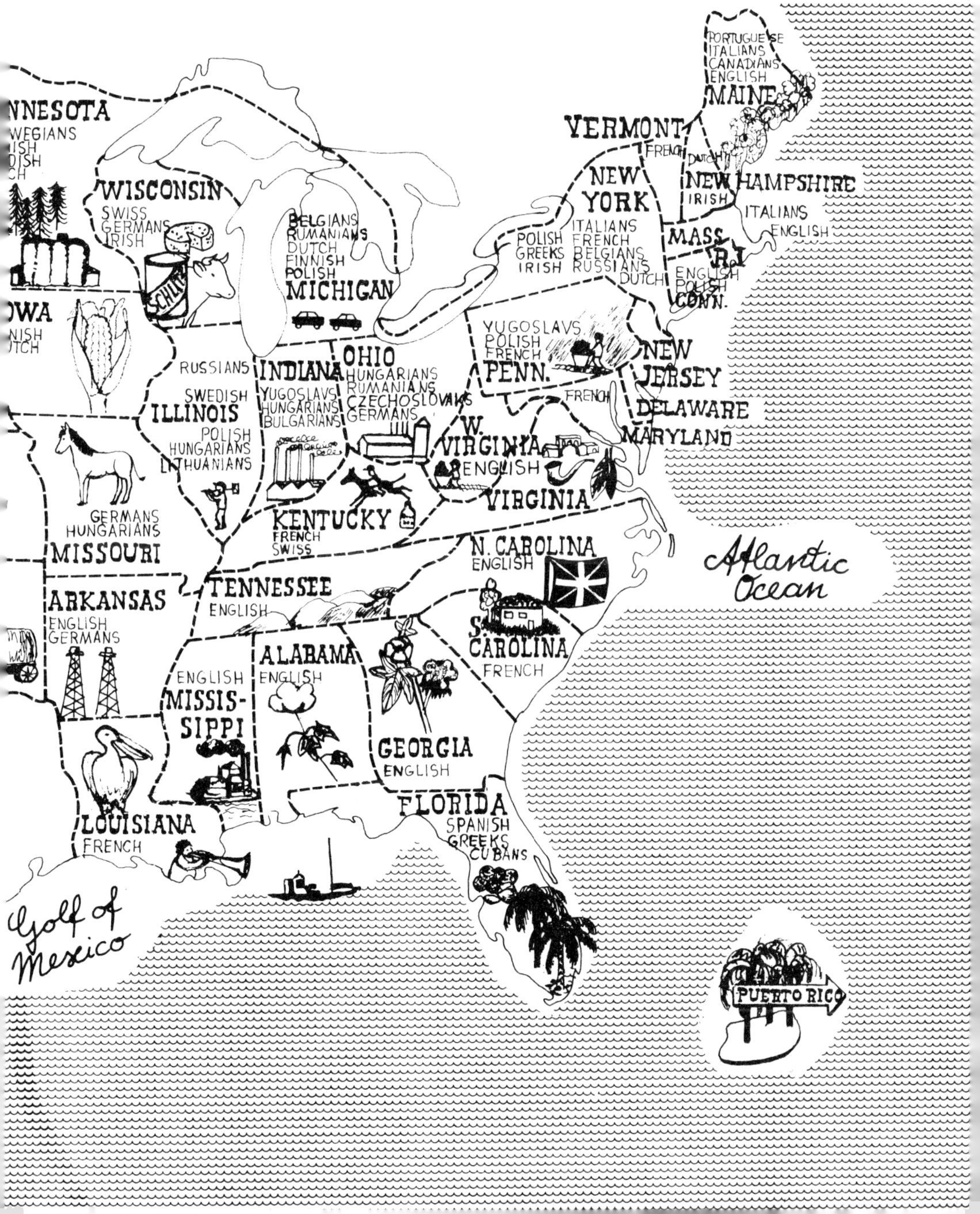

1: DUDLEY RANDALL: The Melting Pot

Dudley Randall (1914–   ), founder, editor, and guiding spirit of Broadside Press in Detroit, the leading Black poetry publishing press in the United States, has been an active force in the development of contemporary Black poetry.

The following poem is from *Cities Burning* (Detroit: Broadside Press, 1968), pp. 322–223, the first collection of Dudley Randall's poetry.

There is a magic melting pot
where any girl or man
can step in Czech or Greek or Scot,
step out American.

Johann and *Jan* and *Jean* and *Juan,*
Giovanni and *Ivan*
step in and then step out again
all freshly christened *John.*

Sam, watching, said, "Why, I was here
even before they came."
and stepped in too, but was tossed out
before he passed the brim.

And every time Sam tried that pot
they threw him out again.
"Keep out. This is our private pot.
We don't want your black stain."

At last, thrown out a thousand times,
Sam said, "I don't give a damn.
Shove your old pot. You can like it or not,
but I'll be just what I am."

(Introduction) 1 *founder* (n.): person who founds or establishes a school, etc. 3 **contemporary** (adj.) /kən`tempə rerɪ/: of the time or period to which reference is being made.

8 **christen** (v.) /`krɪsn/: give a name to at the baptism 12 *brim* (n.): edge of a cup, bowl, glass, etc. 19 *shove* (v.) /ʃʌv/: (taboo) shove (push) s. th. up one's ass. This slang expression indicates refusal and anger on the part of the person who uses it.

2: MICHEL-GUILLAUME JEAN DE CRÈVECŒUR: What Is an American?

Michel-Guillaume Jean de Crèvecœur (1735–1813), known as J. Hector St. John de Crèvecœur, was born in France, and emigrated to Canada during the last of the French and Indian Wars (1754–60). He served under Montcalm and after 1765 settled with his American wife in Orange County, New York. He introduced the culture of European crops in America. He spent idyllic years on his New York farm until the Revolution, when, as a Loyalist, he was forced to flee to New York and then to France (1780). During the quiet decade prior to the Revolution, he probably wrote most of *The Letters from an American Farmer: Written for the Information of a Friend in England* (1782), from which "What Is an American?" is taken.

The following passage is from Henry Steele Commager and Allan Nevins, eds., *The Heritage of America* (Boston: Little, Brown and Co., 1947), pp. 351–355.

I wish I could be acquainted with the feelings and thoughts which must agitate the heart and present themselves to the mind of an enlightened Englishman when he first lands on this continent. He must greatly rejoice that he lived at a time to see this fair country discovered and settled. He must necessarily feel a share of national pride when he views the chain of settlements which embellish these extended shores. Here he sees the industry of his native country displayed in a new manner, and traces, in their works, the embryos of all the arts, sciences, and ingenuity which flourish in Europe. Here he beholds fair cities, substantial villages, extensive fields, an immense country filled with decent houses, good roads, orchards, meadows, and bridges, where, a hundred years ago, all was wild, wooded, and uncultivated! What a train of pleasing ideas this fair spectacle must suggest! It is a prospect which must inspire a good citizen with the most heart-felt pleasure!

The difficulty consists in the manner of viewing so extensive a scene. He is arrived on a new continent; a modern society offers itself to his contemplation, different from what he had hitherto seen. It is not composed, as in Europe, of great lords who possess

---

(Introduction) 2 **emigrate** (v.): go away from one's own country to another to settle there 5 *idyllic* (adj.) /ɪ`dɪlɪk/: simple and pleasant; idyllisch 7 **decade** (n.) /`dekeɪd/: period of ten years 7 *prior to* (prep.) /`praiə/: before.

2 *enlighten* (v.): give more knowledge to; free from ignorance, misunderstanding or false beliefs; aufklären 5 *embellish* (v.): make beautiful; add ornaments or details to 6 **trace** (v.): follow or discover s. th. by observing marks, tracks, etc. 7 *embryo* (n.) /`embrɪəʊ/: s. th. in its rudimentary stage 7 **ingenuity** (n.) /ˈɪndʒɪ`njuətɪ/: cleverness and skill; originality in design 8 *behold* (v.): (old or literary use) take notice, see 8 **substantial** (adj.): large; possessing considerable property 9 **decent** (adj.): right and suitable 11 *prospect* (n.) /`prospekt/: wide view over land or sea 12 *heart-felt* (adj.): sincere 13 *he is arrived*: (archaic for) he has arrived 15 *hitherto* (adv.) /ˈhɪðə`tu/: until now.

everything and of a herd of people who have nothing. Here are no aristocratical families, no courts, no kings, no bishops, no ecclesiastical dominion, no invisible power giving to a few a very visible one, no great manufactures employing thousands, no great refinements of luxury. The rich and the poor are not so far removed from each other as they are in Europe. Some few towns excepted, we are all tillers of the earth, from Nova Scotia to West Florida. We are a people of cultivators, scattered over an immense territory, communicating with each other by means of good roads and navigable rivers, united by the silken bands of mild government, all respecting the laws without dreading their power, because they are equitable. We are all animated with the spirit of an industry which is unfettered and unrestrained, because each person works for himself. If he travels through our rural districts, he views not the hostile castle and the haughty mansion contrasted with the clay-built hut and the miserable cabin where cattle and men help to keep each other warm and dwell in meanness, smoke, and indigence. A pleasing uniformity of decent competence appears throughout our habitations. The meanest of our log houses is a dry and comfortable habitation. Lawyer or merchant are the fairest titles our towns afford; that of a farmer is the only appellation of the rural inhabitants of our country. It must take some time ere he can reconcile himself to our dictionary, which is but short in words of dignity and names of honor. There, on a Sunday, he sees a congregation of respectable farmers and their wives, all clad in neat homespun, well mounted, or riding in their own humble wagons. There is not among them an esquire, saving the unlettered magistrate. There he sees a parson as simple as his flock, a farmer who does not riot on the labor of others. We have no princes for whom we toil, starve, and bleed. We are the most perfect society now existing in the world. Here man is free as he ought to be; nor is this pleasing equality so transitory as many others are. Many ages will not see the shores of our great lakes replenished with inland nations, nor the unknown bounds of North America entirely peopled. Who can tell how far it extends? Who can tell the millions of men whom it will feed and contain, for no European foot has, as yet, traveled half the extent of this mighty continent?

The next wish of this traveler will be to know whence came all these people. They are a mixture of English, Scotch, Irish, French, Dutch, Germans, and Swedes. From

---

16 *aristocratical* (adj.) /ˈærɪstəˋkrætɪkl/: of the aristocracy; having the ways and manners of an aristocrat 17 *ecclesiastical* (adj.) /ɪˈklizɪˋæstɪkl/: of the Christian Church; of clergymen 17 *dominion* (n.): authority to rule; control over 18 **manufacture** (n.) /ˈmænjʊˋfæktʃə(r)/: a firm producing goods on a large scale 19 *refinement* (n.): purity of feeling, taste, language, etc. 20 *tiller* (n.): person who cultivates land 23 *navigable* (adj.) /ˋnævɪgəbl/: suitable for ships 24 *equitable* (adj.) /ˋekwɪtəbl/: fair; just 24/25 *animate* (v.): inspire 25 *fetter* (v.): (fig.) restrain 26 **rural** (adj.): in, of, characteristic of the countryside 27 *haughty* (adj.): arrogant 29 *indigence* (n.) /ˋɪndɪdʒəns/: poverty 29 *competence* (n.): sufficient means for one's needs 30 *habitation* (n.): place to live in 30 *log house* (n.): house with walls and roof made of bulky pieces of timber (not boards) 32 *appellation* (n.): (formal) name or title 33 *ere* (conj.) /ɪə(r)/: (old use) before 33 *reconcile oneself to s. th.* (v.): overcome one's objections to s. th. 33 **but** (adv.): only 34 **congregation** (n.): body of people taking part in religious worship 35 *clad*: (old form) clothed, dressed 35 *homespun* (n.): cloth made of yarn made at home 35 *mounted* (p.p. of mount): beritten 36 *esquire* (n.): in England, a member of the gentry ranking just below the knight; a landed country gentleman, a squire 37 *unlettered* (adj.): uneducated; unable to read 37 *magistrate* (n.) /ˈmædʒɪstreɪt/: minor judge or judicial officer 38 *riot* (v.): live wantonly, revel 40 **transitory** (adj.) /ˋtrænsɪˈtɔrɪ/: temporary; not enduring or permanent 41 *replenish* (v.): fill up again 43 **contain** (v.): be capable of holding.

EQUAL TO ANY IN THE WORLD!!!
MAY BE PROCURED

At FROM $8 to $12 PER ACRE.

Near Markets, Schools, Railroads, Churches, and all the blessings of Civilization.

1,200,000 Acres, in Farms of 40, 80, 120, 160 Acres and upwards, in ILLINOIS, the Garden State of America.

This is how people were lured to emigrate.

this promiscuous breed, that race now called Americans have arisen. The eastern provinces must indeed be excepted, as being the unmixed descendants of Englishmen. I have heard many wish that they had been more intermixed also; for my part, I am no wisher, and think it much better as it has happened. They exhibit a most conspicuous figure in this great and variegated picture. They too enter for a great share in the pleasing perspective displayed in these thirteen provinces. I know it is fashionable to reflect on them, but I respect them for what they have done, for the activity and wisdom with which they have settled their territory, for the decency of their manners, for their early love of letters, their ancient college, the first in this hemisphere, for their industry, which to me, who am but a farmer, is the criterion of everything. There never was a people, situated as they are, who with so ungrateful

---

47 *promiscuous* (adj.) /prə`mɪskjʊəs/: of all sorts of kinds 51 **conspicuous** (adj.) /kən`spɪkjʊəs/: remarkable; attracting attention 51 *variegated* (adj.) /`veərɪgeɪtɪd/: having variety 52 *thirteen provinces*: the thirteen colonies of British North America that joined the American Revolution and became the United States 55 **letters** (pl. n.): literature and learning 55 *ancient college*: Harvard University, the first North American institution of higher learning, founded in 1636 56 **hemisphere** (n.) /`hemɪsfɪə(r)/: half of a sphere or globe; this term has for a long time been used as a name for the American continent ("this hemisphere" or "the western hemisphere"); in the famous *Monroe Doctrine* (1823) it is stated "that we should consider any attempt on their [the European powers'] part to extend their system to any portion of this hemisphere as dangerous to our peace and safety." 56 **criterion** (n.) /kraɪ`tɪərɪən/: principle by which s. th. is measured for value; Kriterium 57 *situated* (pred. adj.): (of a person) in certain circumstances.

a soil have done more in so short a time. Do you think that the monarchical ingredients which are more prevalent in other governments have purged them from all foul stains? Their histories assert the contrary.

In this great American asylum the poor of Europe have by some means met together, and in consequence of various causes. To what purpose should they ask one another what countrymen they are? Alas, two-thirds of them had no country. Urged by a variety of motives, here they came. Everything has tended to regenerate them. New laws, a new mode of living, a new social system. Here they are become men. In Europe they were as so many useless plants, wanting vegetative mold and refreshing showers. They withered and were mowed down by want, hunger, and war; but now, by the power of transplantation, like all other plants, they have taken root and flourished! Formerly they were not numbered in any civil lists of their country except in those of the poor; here they rank as citizens. By what invisible power has this surprising metamorphosis been performed? By that of the laws and that of their industry. The laws, the indulgent laws, protect them as they arrive, stamping on them the symbol of adoption; they receive ample rewards for their labors; these accumulated rewards procure them land; those lands confer on them the title of freemen, and to that title every benefit is affixed which men can possibly require. This is the great operation daily performed by our laws.

What attachment can a poor European emigrant have for a country where he had nothing? The knowledge of the language, the love of a few kindred as poor as himself, were the only cords that tied him. His country is now that which gives him his land, bread, protection, and consequence. . . . What then is the American, this new man? He is neither a European nor the descendant of a European; hence that strange mixture of blood which you will find in no other country. I could point out to you a family whose grandfather was an Englishman, whose wife was Dutch, whose son married a French woman, and whose present four sons have now four wives of different nations. He is an American who, leaving behind him all his ancient prejudices and manners, receives new ones from the new mode of life he has embraced, the new government he obeys, and the new rank he holds. He becomes an American by being received in the broad lap of our great *alma mater*. Here individuals

---

59 **ingredient** (n.): one of the parts of a mixture 59 *prevalent* (adj.) /ˋprevələnt/: common, seen or done everywhere (at the time in question) 59 *purge* (v.): make clean or free 61 **asylum** (n.) /əˋsaɪləm/: (place of) refuge or safety 64 *regenerate* (v.): give new strength or life to 65 *they are become*: (archaic for) they have become 66 *vegetative* (adj.): capable of causing growth in plants 66 **mold** (n.): BE mould; soft, fine loose earth, esp. from decayed vegetable matter; Mutterboden 67 **mow** (v.) /məʊ/: (fig.) cut down like grass; mähen 68 **transplantation** (n.): the taking up of plants with their roots and planting them in another place 71 **metamorphosis** (n.) /ˈmetəˋmɔfəsɪs/: change of form or character 72 *indulgent* (ad.): inclined to give satisfaction or be kind 73 **ample** (adj.): sufficient; plentiful 73/74 **accumulate** (v.): make greater in number 74 **confer** (v.): give or grant (a degree, title) 74 *freeman* (n.): person who has full civil and political rights 75 *affix* (v.): attach 77 **emigrant** (n.): person who leaves his own country for another to settle there 78 *kindred* (n.): relationship by birth between persons 80 *consequence* (n.): importance 86 **prejudice** (n.) /ˋpredʒədɪs/: opinion, like or dislike, formed before one has adequate knowledge or experience 86 *mode* (n.): way in which s. th. is done 87 *embrace* (v.): accept 88 *alma mater* (n.): (from the Latin "bounteous mother") name used for the school or university that one attended.

of all nations are melted into a new race of men whose labors and posterity will one day cause great changes in the world. Americans are the western pilgrims, who are carrying along with them the great mass of arts, sciences, vigor, and industry which began long since in the East. They will finish the great circle. The Americans were once scattered all over Europe. Here they are incorporated into one of the finest systems of population which has ever appeared and which will hereafter become distinct by the power of the different climates they inhabit. The American ought therefore to love this country much better than that in which either he or his forefathers were born. Here the rewards of his industry follow with equal steps the progress of his labor. His labor is founded on the basis of nature, *self-interest*: can it want a stronger allurement? Wives and children, who before in vain demanded of him a morsel of bread, now, fat and frolicsome, gladly help their father to clear those fields whence exuberant crops are to rise, to feed and to clothe them all, without any part being claimed either by a despotic prince, a rich abbot, or a mighty lord. Here religion demands but little of him – a small voluntary salary to the minister, and gratitude to God – can he refuse these? The American is a new man who acts on new principles; he must therefore entertain new ideas and form new opinions. From involuntary idleness, servile dependence, penury, and useless labor, he has passed to toils of a very different nature, rewarded by ample subsistence.

This is an American.

---

90 **the western pilgrims:** the persons who came to Massachusetts on the *Mayflower* in 1620 are called "pilgrims" or "pilgrim fathers". The name "pilgrims" came to be applied to those Puritans who opposed episcopal jurisdiction and the rites of the Church of England and emigrated to America. The New England Pilgrims interpreted their "pilgrimage" to the New World in analogy to the exodus of the Israelites from Egypt to the Promised Land (Canaan). 92 *the great circle*: according to some philosophers of history, the history of civilization must be viewed in terms of a geographical movement from the East to the West 93 *incorporate* (v.): make united in one body or group 95 *different climates*: the influence of the climate on the social system of different nations had already been stressed by the French political philosopher Montesquieu in his *L'Esprit des Lois* (1748). 98 *self-interest* (n.): one's own interests and personal advantage; Eigennutz 99 **allurement** (n.): attraction; that which tempts 99 *morsel* (n.): tiny piece (esp. of food) 100 *frolicsome* (adj.): playful and merry 100 *clear* (v.): to remove so as to leave a cleared space 101 *exuberant* (adj.) /ɪgˈzjubərənt/: growing vigorously 102 *despotic* (adj.): of or like a ruler with unlimited powers, esp. one who uses these powers wrongly or cruelly 102 *abbot* (n.): man at the head of the monks in an abbey or monastery 103 **voluntary** (adj.) /ˈvolənˌterɪ/: without being compelled 103 **minister** (n.): priest or clergyman, esp. one in the Presbyterian and Nonconformist Churches 105 *entertain* (v.): be ready to consider 106 *servile* (adj.): of or like a slave 106 *penury* (n.) /ˈpenjʊərɪ/: (formal) poverty 107 *subsistence* (n.): means of existing.

3: EMMA LAZARUS: The New Colossus

Emma Lazarus (1849–1887) was a New York poet. Her love of the United States as a refuge for the oppressed is expressed in her sonnet to the Statue of Liberty, which was carved on the pedestal of the statue. The Statue of Liberty was presented to the U. S. in 1884 by the Franco-American Union. It commemorates the alliance of France and America during the American revolution.

The poem is taken from Max J. Herzberg, ed., *This Is America* (New York: Pocket Books, Inc., 1951), pp. 74–75.

Not like the brazen giant of Greek fame,
With conquering limbs astride from land to land;
Here at our sea-washed, sunset gates shall stand
A mighty woman with a torch, whose flame
Is the imprisoned lightning, and her name
Mother of Exiles. From her beacon-hand
Glows world-wide welcome; her mild eyes command
The air-bridged harbor that twin cities frame.
"Keep, ancient lands, your storied pomp!" cries she
With silent lips. "Give me your tired, your poor,
Your huddled masses yearning to breathe free,
The wretched refuse of your teeming shore.
Send these, the homeless, tempest-tost to me,
I lift my lamp beside the golden door!"

(Title) *colossus* (n.): immense statue, much greater than life-size; cf. the Colossus of Rhodes, which the ancient Greeks regarded as one of the "Seven Wonders of the World".

(Introduction) 2 **sonnet** (n.): kind of poem containing 14 lines, each of 10 syllables, and written with a formal pattern of rhymes 3 *pedestal* (n.) /ˋpedɪstl/: base for a statue or other work of art; Sockel 4 **commemorate** (v.) /kəˋmeməreɪt/: keep or honour the memory of (a person or event) 5 *alliance* (n.) /əˋlaɪəns/: association; Bündnis.

1 *brazen* (adj.): made of brass; ehern 2 *astride* (pred.adj.): breitbeinig 4 *torch* (n.): a flaming light; Fackel 5 *imprison* (v.): put or keep in prison 6 **exile** (n.) /ˋegzaɪl/: person who has been sent away from his country or home 6 *beacon* (n.): light to give warning of danger or for the guidance of ships; Leuchtfeuer, Bake 7 *command* (v.): be in a position that overlooks (and may control); beherrschen 8 *twin cities*: allusion to the burroughs (Stadtbezirke) of Brooklyn and Manhattan, which are separated by the East River (cf. map on page 85) 9 *storied* (adj.): made famous in legends or stories 9 *pomp* (n.): splendid display 11 **huddle** (v.): crowd together 11 **yearn** (v.): long for 12 **refuse** (n.) /ˋrefjus/: waste or worthless material; Abfall 12 *teem* (v.): be present in large numbers; wimmeln 13 *tempest* (n.): violent storm 13 *tost*: (archaic for) tossed.

"Give me your tired, your poor, your huddled masses yearning to breathe free"

This 1946 Herblock cartoon shows President Harry Truman, Undersecretary of State Dean Acheson, and a bewildered congressman.

"What happened to the one we used to have?"

4: IMMIGRANT BALLAD: No Irish Need Apply

The Irish and German immigrants of the many who came to the New World before 1860, because of their great number, were the most discriminated against by the "native population". There was need for cheap labor in the industrial north. Employers eagerly courted millions of workers from the Old World. Prospective immigrants were tempted by glowing prospectuses of ship companies and railroad agents.

After the uprising of 1798, Ireland was an exploited country. Irish tenants worked on five-acre to fifteen-acre patches of estates belonging to English absentee landlords, and with the decline of prices (after Napoleon's defeat) there was no reason to stay on the land. Even before the potato blight of 1845 about one million Irishmen had arrived in the United States. The potato famine of 1845 set in motion another huge wave of Irish emigration to America. Then the repeal of the Corn Laws (1846) against foreign competition caused the eviction of countless Irish tenants, who for $ 20 a head steerage shipped to the United States. In many cases, the landlords decided that it was cheaper to hire local immigrants, who stayed in the neighborhoods of relatives and friends. Soon Boston and New York became slum-ridden with immigrants living in ghettos. Employers began to discriminate and the "No Irish Need Apply" notation which accompanied many job advertisements became a source of bitter resentment. The immigrants began to publish their own newspapers, form their own volunteer militia, and the cities were divided into unfriendly national groups. The "native population" became frightened and organized protective societies, which became political clubs and helped form the "Know-Nothing" or American Party. The depression of 1857 added to the great number of unemployed, who in New York numbered over 40,000.

This immigrant song is taken from *Frontier Ballads* (Folkways Records, New York, Album No. FA 2175, Sung by Pete Seeger with Five String Banjo).

(Title) **immigrant** (adj.): of or having to do with immigrants (persons coming into another country to settle there) *apply* (v.): (formally) ask for; sich bewerben.

(Introduction) 2 **discriminate against** (v.): treat differently 5 *prospectus* (n.): printed account giving details of and advertising s. th. 6 *agent* (n.): person who acts for, or who manages the business affairs of another or others 7 **uprising** (n.): revolt; rebellion 7 **exploit** (v.): use selfishly, or for one's own profit; ausbeuten 7 **tenant** (n.): person who pays rent for the use of land, a building, etc. 9 *absentee landlord* (n.) /ˈæbsnˋti/: landowner who habitually lives away from the place where his land is 10 *blight* (n.): any insect, disease, etc. that destroys plants 11 **famine** (n.) /ˋfæmɪn/: extreme scarcity of food in a region; Hungersnot 13 **repeal** (n.): revocation; abrogation; Aufhebung 14 **eviction** (n.): expelling a tenant from a house or land by authority of the law 14 **steerage** (n.): that part of a ship nearest the rudder; this section formerly used for providing for passengers travelling at the lowest fares; Zwischendeck 16 **neighborhood** (n.): a particular community, district, or area 18 *ghetto* (n.): any section of a city in which many members of a minority group live 19 *notation* (n.): a brief note or noting 20 **resentment** (n.): bitter feeling 21 *volunteer militia* (n.) /mɪˋlɪʃə/: force of civilians who are trained as soldiers but not part of the regular army; Freiwilligenmiliz.

Eviction of Irish peasants, 1848. Backed by the military, the landlord's agents tear down a family's cottage to make way for large-scale farming.

23 *"Know-Nothing" or American Party*: During the 1840s in Eastern cities where Roman Catholic immigrants especially had concentrated and been welcomed by Democrats, local nativistic societies formed to combat "foreign" influences and uphold the "American" view. The Native American Party became a national party in 1845. In the 1850s many secret orders grew up. All inquiries of supposed members were met with a statement to the effect that they knew nothing; hence members were called Know-Nothings. In 1855 they adopted the name American Party. 24 **depression** (n.): period of reduced business, much unemployment, etc.; Wirtschaftskrise.

I'm a decent boy just landed
From the town of Balyfad;
I want a situation yes,
And I want it very bad.

I seen employment advertised
It's just the thing says I;
But the dirty spalpeen ended with
No Irish need apply.

O, says I, but that's an insult
O, to get the place I'll try;
So I went to see the blackguard
With his no Irish need apply.

Some do think it a misfortune
To be christened Pat or Dan;
But to me it is an honor
To be born an Irishman.

I started out to find the house,
I got it mighty soon;
There I found the old chap seated,
He was reading the Tribune.

I told him what I came for,
When he in a rage did fly;
NO, he says, you are a Paddy and
No Irish need apply.

Well, I gets my dander rising,
I would like to black his eye
To tell an Irish gentleman
No Irish need apply.

Some do think it a misfortune
To be christened Pat or Dan;
But to me it is an honor
To be born an Irishman.

I couldn't stand it longer
So a-hold of him I took;
I gave him such a welting
As he'd get at Donnybrook.

He hollered Milia Murther
And to get away did try;
And swore he'd never write again
No Irish need apply.

O, he makes a big apology
I bid him then goodby;
Saying when next you want a beating, you write
No Irish need apply.

Some do think it a misfortune
To be christened Pat or Dan;
But to me it is an honor
To be born an Irishman.

---

1 **decent** (adj.): respectful 2 *Balyfad* (n.): small town in Ireland, near Cork 3 *situation* (n.): work, employment 4 *bad* (adv.): sl. for badly 5 *I seen*: sl. for I saw 6 *says I*: sl. for say I 7 *spalpeen* (n.): (Irish dial.) low or mean fellow 11 *blackguard* (n.): /ˈblægɑd/: dishonest person; Schurke 14 **christen** (v.) /ˈkrɪsn/: give a name to at the baptism 18 *mighty* (adv.): sl. for very 20 *Tribune* (n.): New York Tribune, a daily newspaper founded in 1841 23 *Paddy* (n.): (nickname for an) Irishman 25 *I gets*: (uneducated for) I get 25 *dander* (n.): (coll.) anger or temper 34 *take a-hold of*: (sl. and ballad style) take hold of 35 *welt* (v.): beat down 36 *Donnybrook* (n.): small town southeast of Cork, Ireland 37 *holler* (v.): (coll.) shout; yell 37 *Milia Murther*: Zetermordio; wehklagendes Geschrei 41 **apology** (n.): statement of regret; Entschuldigung 42 *bid, bid, bid* (v.): say (as a greeting, etc.).

5: NEW YORK STATE COMMISSIONERS OF EMIGRATION: The Perils of the Crossing

For a long time, the difficulties of the voyage between Europe and America exerted a deep influence upon all immigrants. Death claimed many who left their homes with hope in their hearts; and fear of the dangers kept others at home. But even those who came safely off the ships for years thereafter were marked by the trying experience. As if the perils of the ocean and the weather were not enough, the passengers were also at the mercy of greedy captains and shipowners. In the early years, when many immigrants had signed contracts as servants (and had thus gained the status of "indentured servants") in return for free passage to America, they were subject to ruthless exploitation. But in 1868 the New York State Commissioners of Emigration revealed that even free passengers who paid their own way were helpless. Toward the end of the nineteenth century, the steamship shortened the length of the journey and mitigated some of its perils.

The following report by the New York State Commissioners of Emigration is taken from Oscar Handlin, *Immigration as a Factor in American History* (Englewood Cliffs, N. J.: Prentice-Hall, 1959), pp. 34–38.

The *Leibnitz,* originally the *Van Couver,* is a large and fine vessel, built at Boston for the China trade, and formerly plying between that port and China. She was sold some years ago to the house of Robert M. Sloman, and has since sailed under her present name.

We were informed that her last trip was her second with emigrants on board. Last summer, she went to Quebec with about seven hundred passengers, of whom she lost only a few on her passage; this time, she left Hamburg, November 2, 1867, Capt. H. F. Bornhold, lay at Cuxhaven, on account of head-winds, until the 11th,

---

(Introduction) 2 **exert** (v.) /ɪg`zɛt/: bring into use; ausüben 6 **greedy** (adj.): wanting more than one needs or deserves; gierig 7 **immigrant** (n.): person who comes as a settler into another country 8 *indenture* (v.): bind a person (e. g. an apprentice, a servant) by a written agreement to a master 9 *subject* (adj.): exposed 9 **ruthless** (adj.): cruel; without pity 9 **exploitation** (n.): making unethical use for one's own profit; Ausbeutung 10 *commissioner* (n.): member of a body of persons given the duty of making an inquiry and writing a report 10 **emigration** (n.): going away from one's own country to another to settle there 13 *mitigate* (v.): make less severe, violent or painful; lindern.

2 *ply* (v.): (of ships, busses, etc.) go regularly to and fro 8 *on account of* (prep.): because of 8 *head-wind* (n.): wind that blows directly into one's face, or against the course of a ship.

whereupon she took the southern course to New York. She went by the way of Madeira, down to the Tropics, 20th degree, and arrived in the Lower Bay on January 11, 1868, after a passage of 61 days, or rather 70 days – at least, as far as the passengers are concerned, who were confined to the densely crowded steerage for that length of time.

The heat, for the period that they were in the lower latitudes, very often reached 24 degrees of Réaumur, or 94 degrees of Fahrenheit. Her passengers 544 in all – of whom 395 were adults, 103 children, and 46 infants – came principally from Mecklenburg, and proposed to settle as farmers and laborers in Illinois and Wisconsin; besides them, there were about 40 Prussians from Pomerania and Posen, and a few Saxons and Thuringians. . . .

Of these 544 German passengers, 105 died on the voyage, and three in port, making in all 108 deaths – leaving 436 surviving.

The first death occurred on November 25th. On some days, as for instance on December 1, nine passengers died, and on December 17, eight. The sickness did not abate until toward the end of December, and no new cases happened when the ship had again reached the northern latitudes. Five children were born. During the voyage some families had died out entirely; of others, the fathers or mothers are gone; here, a husband had left a poor widow, with small children; and there, a husband had lost his wife. We spoke to some little boys and girls, who, when asked where were their parents, pointed to the ocean with sobs and tears, and cried, *"Down there!"*

Prior to our arrival on board, the ship had been cleansed and fumigated several times, but not sufficiently so to remove the dirt, which, in some places, covered the walls. Mr. Frederick Kassner, our able and experienced Boarding Officer, reports that he found the ship and the passengers in a most filthy condition, and that when boarding the *Leibnitz* he hardly discovered a clean spot on the ladder, or on the ropes, where he could put his hands and feet. He does not remember to have seen anything like it within the last five years. . . .

As to the interior of the vessel, the upper steerage is high and wide. All the spars, beams, and planks which were used for the construction of temporary berths had been removed. Except through two hatchways and two very small ventilators, it had no

---

12 **steerage** (n.): that part of a ship nearest the rudder; this section formerly used for providing for passengers travelling at the lowest fares; Zwischendeck 14 *latitude* (n.): distance north or south of the equator measured in degrees; Breitengrad 15 *Réaumur* (n.): designating or of a temperature scale which registers the boiling point of water at 80° and the freezing point at 0° 15 *Fahrenheit* (n.) /ˈfærənhaɪt/: name of a thermometer scale with freezing point at 32° and boiling point at 212°; to convert Fahrenheit temperature into Centigrade (Celsius) substract 32 and multiply by 5/9 (five ninths) 16 **infant** (n.): child during the first few years of its life 24 *abate* (v.): become less 31 *prior to* (prep.): before 31 **cleanse** (v.) /ˈklenz/: make thoroughly clean 31 *fumigate* (v.): disinfect by means of strong-smelling smoke or gas 34 **filthy** (adj.): disgustingly dirty 38 *spar* (n.): strong wooden or metal pole used as a mast, yard, boom, etc. 39 *plank* (n.): long, flat piece of timber 40 *hatchway* (n.): movable covering in a ship's deck through which cargo is lowered and raised.

Dreaming the American Dream?

ventilation, and not a single window or bull's-eye was open during the voyage. In general, however, it was not worse than the average of the steerages of other emigrant ships; but the lower steerage, the so-called orlop-deck, is a perfect pesthole, calculated to kill the healthiest man. It had been made a temporary room for the voyage by laying a tier of planks over the lower beams of the vessel, and they were so supported that they shook when walking on them. The little light this orlop-deck received came through one of the hatchways of the upper-deck. Although the latter was open when we were on board, and although the ship was lying in the open sea, free from all sides, it was impossible to see anything at a distance of two or three feet.

---

43 *orlop-deck* (n.): lowest deck of a ship 43 *pesthole* (n.): metaphor for a place in which an epidemic disease (pestilence) occurs 45 *tier* (n.) /tɪə(r)/: row 49 *foot* (n.): measure of length; 1 foot=30, 479 cm.

On our enquiring how this hole had been lighted during the voyage, we were told that some lanterns had been up there, but on account of the foulness of the air, they could scarcely burn. It had, of course, much less than the upper-deck draft or ventilation, and was immediately over the keel, where the bilge-water collects, and adjoining part of the cargo, which consisted of wool and hides. And in this place about 120 passengers were crowded for 70 days, and for a greater part of the voyage in a tropical heat, with scanty rations and a very inadequate supply of water, and worse than all, suffering from the miasma below, above, and beside them, which of itself must create fever and pestilence!

The captain himself stated to us that the passengers refused to carry the excrements on the deck, and that "the urine and ordure of the upper-steerage flowed down to the lower." As the main-deck was very difficult of access from the orlop-deck, the inmates of the latter often failed to go on deck even to attend to the calls of nature. There were only six water-closets for the accommodation of all the passengers. They have been cleansed, of course; but the smell that emanated from them was still very intense, and corroborates the statement of the above-named officers – that they must have been in an extraordinary frightful condition.

When the ship *Lord Brougham,* belonging to the same line, arrived on the 6th of December last, from Hamburg, and had lost 75 out of 383 passengers, we personally examined the majority of the survivors, and found them not only healthy and in good spirits, but, at the same time, in every respect satisfied with the treatment they had received on board.

The present case, however, is different. There was not a single emigrant who did not complain of the captain, as well as of the short allowance of provisions and water on board. As we know, from a long experience, that the passengers of emigrant ships, with a very few exceptions, are in the habit of claiming more than they are entitled to, we are far from putting implicit faith in all their statements. There is as much falsehood and exaggeration among this class of people as among any other body of uneducated men. We have, therefore, taken their complaints with due allowance, and report only so much thereof as we believe to be well founded.

All the passengers concur in the complaint that their provisions were short, partly rotten, and that, especially, the supply of water was insufficient, until they were approaching port. We examined the provisions on board, and found that the water was clear and pure. If the whole supply during the voyage was such as the samples handed to us, there was no reason to complain as to quality. But, in quantity, the

---

50 **enquire** (v.): ask for information about 53 *bilge-water* (n.): the dirty water that collects in a ship's bottom 54 **cargo** (n.): goods carried in a ship, aircraft or other vehicle 54 *hide* (n.): animal's skin, esp. as an article of commerce and manufacture 56 **scanty** (adj.): small in size or amount; barely large enough 56 *ration* (n.): fixed quantity, esp. of food allowed to one person; Ration 57 *miasma* (n.) /mɪˈæzmə/: unhealthy mist rising from the ground, formerly associated with malaria etc. 58 *pestilence* (n.): any kind of fatal epidemic disease 60 *ordure* (n.) /ˈɔdʒə(r)/: excrement; dung; filth 63 *accommodation* (n.): s. th. that helps; s. th. for convenience 64 *emanate* (v.): come, flow, proceed from 65 *corroborate* (v.): give support or certainty to a statement, belief, theory, etc. 73 **allowance** (n.): amount of food, money, etc. given regularly to a person 73 **provisions** (pl. n.): food supplies 76 **implicit** (adj.): implied though not plainly expressed 77 **exaggeration** (n.): Übertreibung 78 **allowance** (n.): excuse because of mitigating (erleichternde) factors 80 *concur* (v.): agree.

complaints of the passengers are too well founded; for they unanimously state, and are not effectually contradicted by the captain, that they never received more than half a pint of drinkable water per day, while by the laws of the United States they were entitled to receive three quarts. Some of the biscuit handed to us were rotten and old, and hardly eatable; other pieces were better. We ordered the steward to open a cask of corned-beef and found it of ordinary good quality. The butter, however, was rancid. Once a week herrings were cooked instead of meat. The beans and sauerkraut were often badly cooked, and, in spite of hunger, thrown overboard.

The treatment of the passengers was heartless in the extreme. The sick passengers received the same food with the healthy, and high prices were exacted for all extras and comforts. A regular traffic in wine, beer, and liquors was carried on between the passengers on the one side and the steward and crew on the other. . . .

When the first deaths occurred, the corpses were often suffered to remain in the steerage for full twenty-four hours. In some cases the bodies were covered with vermin before they were removed.

There was no physician on board. Although we found a large medicine-chest, it was not large enough for the many cases of sickness, and was, in fact, emptied after the first two weeks of the voyage.

The captain seems to have been sadly deficient in energy and authority in matters of moment, while he punished severely small offences; as, for instance, he handcuffed a passenger for the use of insulting words; but he did not enforce the plainest rules for the health and welfare of his passengers. Instead of compelling them, from the first, to come on deck and remove the dirt, he allowed them to remain below, and to perish among their own excrements. Of the whole crew, the cook alone fell sick and died, as he slept in the steerage. Three passenger girls who were employed in the kitchen, and lived on deck, enjoyed excellent health, during the whole voyage.

The physicians . . . to whose report we refer for particulars, most positively declare that it was not the Asiatic cholera, but intestinal and stomach catarrh . . . more or less severe, and contagious typhus, which killed the passengers. From what we saw and learned from the passengers, we likewise arrive at the conclusion that the shocking mortality on board the *Leibnitz* arose from want of good ventilation, cleanliness, suitable medical care, sufficient water, and wholesome food.

---

85 **unanimous** (adj.) /juˈnænɪməs/: showing complete agreement; einhellig 86 *effectual* (adj.): valid 86 **contradict** (v.): deny the truth of s. th. said or written 87 *pint* (n.) /paɪnt/: unit of measure for liquids, one-eighth of a gallon or about 0,57 of a litre 88 *quart* (n.): measure of capacity equal to two pints or about 1, 14 litre 89 *cask* (n.): barrel 90 *rancid* (adj.): having gone bad; ranzig 94 *exact* (v.): demand and enforce payment of 95 *traffic* (n.): illicit trading; unerlaubter Handel 97 **corpse** (n.): dead body of a human being 99 *vermin* (n.): any of various destructive insects or small animals, as lice, rats, etc. 100 *physician* (n.): doctor of medicine 103 **deficient** (adj.): not having enough of 104 *moment* (n.): importance 104 *handcuff* (v.): Handschellen anlegen 105 *enforce* (v.): compel obedience to 112 *intestinal* (adj.): of the lower part of the food canal from below the stomach to the anus 113 **contagious** (adj.): ansteckend 116 *wholesome* (adj.): healthy.

6: UNITED STATES IMMIGRATION COMMISSION: The Immigrant and the Labor Market

The sharpest disputes over the economic effects of immigration came after 1880 with reference to the role of newcomers as industrial laborers. This was one of the subjects of investigation of a federal immigration commission that studied the matter between 1907 and 1910. The following report was made by the United States Immigration Commission, "Reports", 61st Congress, 3rd Session, *Senate Document,* No. 747, I, 37–39.

The text is taken from Oscar Handlin, ed., *Immigration as a Factor in American History* (Englewood Cliffs, N. J.: Prentice-Hall, 1959), pp. 54–56.

A large proportion of the southern and eastern European immigrants of the past twenty-five years have entered the manufacturing and mining industries of the eastern and middle western States, mostly in the capacity of unskilled laborers. There is no basic industry in which they are not largely represented and in many cases they compose more than 50 per cent of the total number of persons employed in such industries. Coincident with the advent of these millions of unskilled laborers there has been an unprecedented expansion of the industries in which they have been employed. Whether this great immigration movement was caused by the industrial development, or whether the fact that a practically unlimited and available supply of cheap labor existed in Europe was taken advantage of for the purpose of expanding the industries, can not well be demonstrated. Whatever may be the truth in this regard it is certain that southern and eastern European immigrants have almost completely monopolized unskilled labor activities in many of the more important industries. This phase of the industrial situation was made the most important and exhaustive feature of the Commission's investigation, and the results show that while the competition of these immigrants has had little, if any, effect on the highly skilled trades, nevertheless, through lack of industrial progress and by reason of large and

---

(Title) **immigrant** (n.): person who comes as a settler into another country.

(Introduction) 1 *dispute* (n.): debate, argument 3 **federal** (adj.): of, based upon, federation; relating to central as distinct from State government.

3 *capacity* (n.): position 3 **unskilled** (adj.): (of workers) not having special skill or special training 4 **basic** (adj.): fundamental 5 *compose* (v.): make up 6 *coincident* (adj.): occurring at the same time 6 *advent* (n.): coming or arrival 7 *unprecedented* (adj.) /ʌnˋpresɪdentɪd/: never done or known before 11 **demonstrate** (v.): show clearly by giving proof or example 13 *monopolize* (v.): /məˋnopəlɑɪz/: control the whole of, so that others cannot share 17 *by reason of* (prep.): because of.

The great coal and steel industries owed much to the immigrant groups, among them the Welsh and the Poles who came to Pennsylvania and Ohio in the nineteenth century. The picture shows a scene in an anthracite mine.

constant reinforcement from abroad, it has kept conditions in the semiskilled and unskilled occupations from advancing.

Several elements peculiar to the new immigrants contributed to this result. The aliens came from countries where low economic conditions prevailed and where conditions of labor were bad. They were content to accept wages and conditions which the native American and immigrants of the older class had come to regard as unsatisfactory. They were not, as a rule, engaged at lower wages than had been paid to the older workmen for the same class of labor, but their presence in constantly increasing numbers prevented progress among the older wage-earning class, and as a result that class of employees was gradually displaced. An instance of this displacement is shown in the experience in the bituminous coal mines of western Pennsylvania. This section of the bituminous field was the one first entered by the new immigrants, and the displacement of the old workers was soon under way. Some of them entered other occupations and many of them migrated to the coal fields of the Middle West. Later these fields also were invaded by the new immigrants, and large numbers of the old workers again migrated to the mines of the Southwest, where they still predominate. The effect of the new immigration is clearly shown in the western Pennsylvania fields, where the average wage of the bituminous coal worker is 42 cents a day

---

18 **reinforcement** (n.): strengthening, as by adding new persons or material 21 **alien** (n.) /ˈeɪlɪən/: a foreign-born resident who is not a citizen 27 **employee** (n.) /ˈemplɔɪˈi/: person given work for payment 27 *displace* (v.): take the place of; put s. b. else in the place of 28 *bituminous* (adj.) /bɪˈtjumɪnəs/: containing a black, sticky substance from petroleum 31 **migrate** (v.) /ˈmaɪgreɪt/: move from one place to another.

below the average wage in the Middle West and the Southwest. Incidentally, hours of labor are longer and general working conditions poorer in the Pennsylvania mines than elsewhere. Another characteristic of the new immigrants contributed to the situation in Pennsylvania. This was the impossibility of successfully organizing them into labor unions. Several attempts at organization were made, but the constant influx of immigrants to whom prevailing conditions seemed unusually favorable contributed to the failure to organize. A similar situation has prevailed in other great industries.

Like most of the immigration from southern and eastern Europe, those who entered the leading industries were largely single men or married men unaccompanied by their families. There is, of course, in practically all industrial communities a large number of families of the various races, but the majority of the employees are men without families here, and whose standard of living is so far below that of the native American or older immigrant workman that it is impossible for the latter to successfully compete with them. They usually live in cooperative groups and crowd together. Consequently, they are able to save a great part of their earnings, much of which is sent or carried abroad. Moreover, there is a strong tendency on the part of these unaccompanied men to return to their native countries after a few years of labor here. These groups have little contact with American life, learn little of American institutions, and aside from the wages earned profit little by their stay in this country. During their early years in the United States they usually rely for assistance and advice on some member of their race, frequently a saloon keeper or grocer, and almost always a steamship ticket agent and "immigrant banker", who, because of superior intelligence and better knowledge of American ways, commands their confidence. Usually after a longer residence they become more self-reliant, but their progress toward assimilation is generally slow. Immigrant families in the industrial centers are more permanent and usually exhibit a stronger tendency toward advancement, although, in most cases, it is a long time before they even approach the ordinary standard of the American or the older immigrant families in the same grade of occupation. This description, of course, is not universally true, but it fairly represents a great part of the recent immigrant population in the United States. Their numbers are so great and the influx is so continuous that even with the remarkable expansion of industry during the past few years there has been created an oversupply of unskilled labor, and in some of the industries this is reflected in a curtailed number of working days and a consequent yearly income among the unskilled workers which is very much less than is indicated by the daily wage rates paid; and while it may not have lowered in a marked degree the American standard of living, it has introduced a lower standard which has become prevalent in the unskilled industry at large.

---

37 **poor** (adj.): AE for BE bad 38 *characteristic* (n.): special mark or quality 41 **influx** (n.): inflow of large numbers or quantities 50 *cooperative* (adj.) /kəʊˋopərətɪv/: sharing together 52 *on the part of*: proceeding from, done by; seitens 57 *saloon* (n.): place where alcoholic drinks may be bought and drunk 69 **curtail** (v.): cut off a part of; beschneiden, kürzen.

7: RICHMOND MAYO-SMITH: Advocating Assimilation*

The sociologist Richmond Mayo-Smith published his influential work *Emigration and Immigration: A Study in Social Science* in 1890. Mayo-Smith holds that American character was already formed and was not to be modified by the immigrants. He makes the point that it is the task of immigrants simply to rid themselves of their old habits and culture in order to become Americans.

The following text is taken from Oscar Handlin, ed., *Immigration as a Factor in American History* (Englewood Cliffs, N. J.: Prentice-Hall, 1959), pp. 159–163.

A much more important subject of study, however, is the effect of this immigration on the ethnical or race composition of our population. If it at present consisted merely of the descendants of the people who were here in 1790, with slight additions from year to year of immigrants from Europe, we should be, with the exception of the blacks, a remarkably homogeneous people. Notwithstanding the fact that among the original colonists were to be found Dutch, Germans, Swedes and French, yet the dominating element was the English. This is seen in the fact that the language has remained English, and that the institutions are English. The long connection of all the colonies with England, whatever the original home of the colonists, accounts for this in large measure. The revolutionary struggle united the people and gave them the feeling of one nationality. Free institutions have worked in the same way, until we find the native-born Americans, however widely separated by distance, exhibiting very much the same traits. In later years the means of communication, the common interest in the common government, and still more the commercial intercourse unhindered by tax-barriers and facilitated by the same language, the same money and similar commercial law have unified the whole. There is less difference in language, customs and feeling between the inhabitants of distant portions of the United States than there is often between counties or provinces of European States, which have had different historical development. This influence has been so strong that it has

---

(Title) **advocate** (v.): support **assimilation** (n.): the act of becoming or making part of another social group or political system.

(Introduction) 1 **emigration** (n.): instance of going away from one's own country to another to settle there 2 **immigration** (n.): instance of coming as a settler into another country 3 *modify* (v.): make different.

2 **ethnical** (adj.): of race 5 **homogeneous** (adj.) /ˈhəʊməˈdʒinɪəs/: (formed of parts) of the same kind 5 *notwithstanding* (prep.): in spite of 7 **dominate** (v.): be most important or influential 14 *intercourse* (n.): exchanges of trade 15 **hinder** (v.): obstruct; get in the way of 15 *barrier* (n.) /ˈbærɪə(r)/: s. th. that prevents, hinders or controls 15 *facilitate* (v.): make easy; lessen the difficulty of 16 **unify** (v.): form into one; make uniform.

enabled us to assimilate many elements of different quality, and has leavened, at least to a certain extent, the whole lump.

But during the last forty years the immigration has been so large that the process of assimilation has become more difficult, and the addition of foreign elements has been so rapid that it has made the race composition of our population essentially different from what it would have been if we had been left to our own natural growth. These foreign elements are now so prominent that it is worth our while to consider the actual composition of our population as it presents itself to-day....

The strength of this foreign element is disclosed if we take a typical state and study the make-up of its population more closely. Massachusetts is commonly thought of as peculiarly an American community, where the population is largely composed of descendants of the Puritans. It was found in 1885 that over 27 per cent of the inhabitants of that commonwealth were of foreign birth, and that over one-half of all the inhabitants were of foreign parentage. Nearly 30 per cent were of Irish parentage alone.

The persons of foreign birth in the United States seem to seek the large cities. In 1880 more than 34 per cent were found therein. Of the Irish, 45 per cent settle in the large cities; of the Germans, 38 per cent; of the English and Scotch, 30 per cent; of the Italians, 60 per cent. In the city of Boston in 1885 only 31 per cent of the inhabitants were of native (i. e. born in the United States) parentage; the rest were of foreign parentage. In the city of Lowell only 30 per cent were of native parentage; in Lawrence, 22 per cent; in Fall River, 17 per cent; and in the city of Holyoke, only 16 per cent. Many of our factory towns and cities are really foreign so far as the nationality of their inhabitants goes.

These statistics show that in certain parts of the country the foreign element in our population has become very powerful and is in fact overshadowing the native. Especially in the cities it shows its strength. But it always tends to concentrate. This is due to several causes. One is that the immigrants naturally seek that portion of the country where they can find employment in their particular trades. The miners from Wales and England naturally go to the mines of Pennsylvania. The lumbermen from Canada seek the forests of the Northern States. The unskilled labor remains in the large city where it is employed in the rougher parts of building trades, or seeks the factory town where it can soon learn to manage the simple operations of industrial machinery. Another great influence is the presence of friends or countrymen upon whom the newly arrived immigrants can depend for help and counsel. Many come at the solicitation of friends or relatives, or with the aid of money sent by them, and naturally go to them on their arrival.

---

20 *leaven* (v.) /ˈlevn/: add a substance (yeast = Hefe) to s. th. and thus causing gradual change 26 *prominent* (adj.): important; easily seen 28 *disclose* (v.): uncover; make known 29 **make-up** (n.): the way s. th. is put together; nature 31 **Puritan** (n.): member of a Protestant group in England and the American colonies who, in the 16th and 17th centuries, wanted a greater reformation of the Church of England than that established by Elisabeth I, so as to purify it further from elaborate ceremonies and forms 33 **parentage** (n.): origin; birth 55 *solicitation* (n.): request.

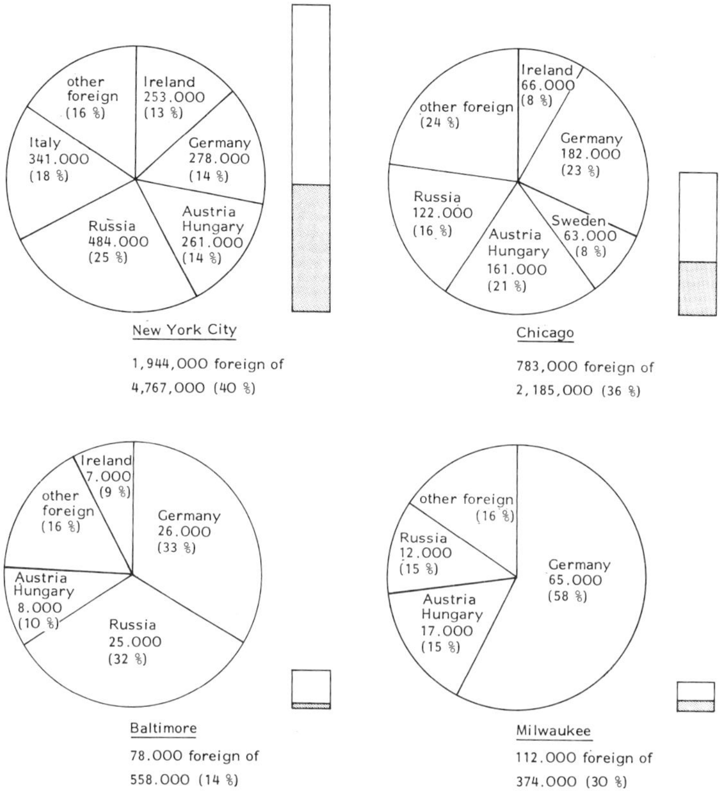

Foreign-born in Cities, 1910

There are, fortunately, certain forces which tend to counteract this exclusiveness on the part of the immigrants and gradually to fuse the different elements into one American nationality. Two of these we have already mentioned, viz., economic prosperity and the practice of free political institutions. The former widens the circle of wants of the new citizen and leads him to imitate the higher style of living which he sees about him. This separates him from the habits and traditions of his native country and he adopts new standards which are associated in his mind with the new domicile, and which produce a feeling of superiority when he revisits the old home or comes into contact with later arrivals. It differentiates him, so to speak, from the immigrant, and gives him a feeling of attachment to the country where he has prospered. This feeling increases with his children and grandchildren until they become fully identified with our customs, manner of living and habits of thought, and are thoroughly Americanized.

58 **fuse** (v.): make into one whole 59 viz. /vɪz/: that is to say; namely; read as "namely" 64 *domicile* (n.) /ˈdomɪsaɪl/: place where one lives permanently 65 **differentiate** (v.) /ˌdɪfəˈrenʃɪeɪt/: show to be different; unterscheiden.

The exercise of political rights, to which many of the immigrants are strange, tends to differentiate them in much the same way. It makes them of importance to the political leaders. It gives them a higher position than they were accustomed to at home, and this naturally attaches them to the new country. However much our politics may suffer from the addition of this vote, much of it ignorant and some of it depraved, there is no doubt as to the educational and nationalizing effect of the suffrage on the immigrants themselves. However attached the Irishman may be to the cause of home rule for Ireland, or however proud the German may be of the military glory of the empire, his feelings must gradually and unconsciously gravitate to the country where he has found economic prosperity and political recognition. He may still observe the national feast days and wave the old flag, but if it ever came to a contest, he would probably find that he was more of an American than an Irishman or a German.

Another great fusing force has been the dominance of one language, – the English. In the great mass of cases the immigrant has found it necessary or desirable to adopt that language. Where he has not done it himself, his children have; and in many cases it has become the mother tongue if not the only tongue of the descendants. As soon as that happens, the man of foreign descent is irreparably separated from his former home. In some cases thickly settled communities have managed to maintain the foreign speech and the old religion for several generations. But the disintegrating forces are at work all about them. The moment the young man ventures out into the world he is obliged to learn English. The moment he aspires to the higher education or to political or commercial position he must recognize the prevailing tongue. The children learn it in the school. The parents recognize that it is desirable for the children if not for themselves. It is impossible to isolate the little community completely and it is gradually undermined.

It is eminently desirable that it should be so. We must have one speech in this country. We must insist that English shall be taught in the schools and that it shall be the fundamental language of future generations. It must be everywhere the official language of the courts and the laws. German clergymen and educated men sometimes regret that the immigrants and their descendants should lose this connection with the old country and access to the great literature of the German tongue. But it is better that a man should have one country and not divide his allegiance. If we are to build up in this country one nationality we must insist upon one speech.

---

75 *depraved* (adj.): morally bad; vicious 75 *nationalize* (v.): make a person a citizen 76 **suffrage** (n.) /ˋsʌfrɪdʒ/: right of voting in political elections 77 *home rule* (n.): government of a country by its own citizens 78 *gravitate* (v.): move or be attracted 83 **dominance** (n.): Vorherrschen 87 *irreparable* (adj.) /ɪˋreprəbl/: that cannot be put right or restored 89 *disintegrate* (v.): (cause to) break up into small parts or pieces 91 **aspire** (v.): be filled with high ambition; streben 94 **isolate** (v.): separate, put or keep apart from others 101 **access** (n.) /ˋækses/: opportunity or means of reaching; Zugang 102 **allegiance** (n.) /əˋlidʒəns/: loyalty to a government.

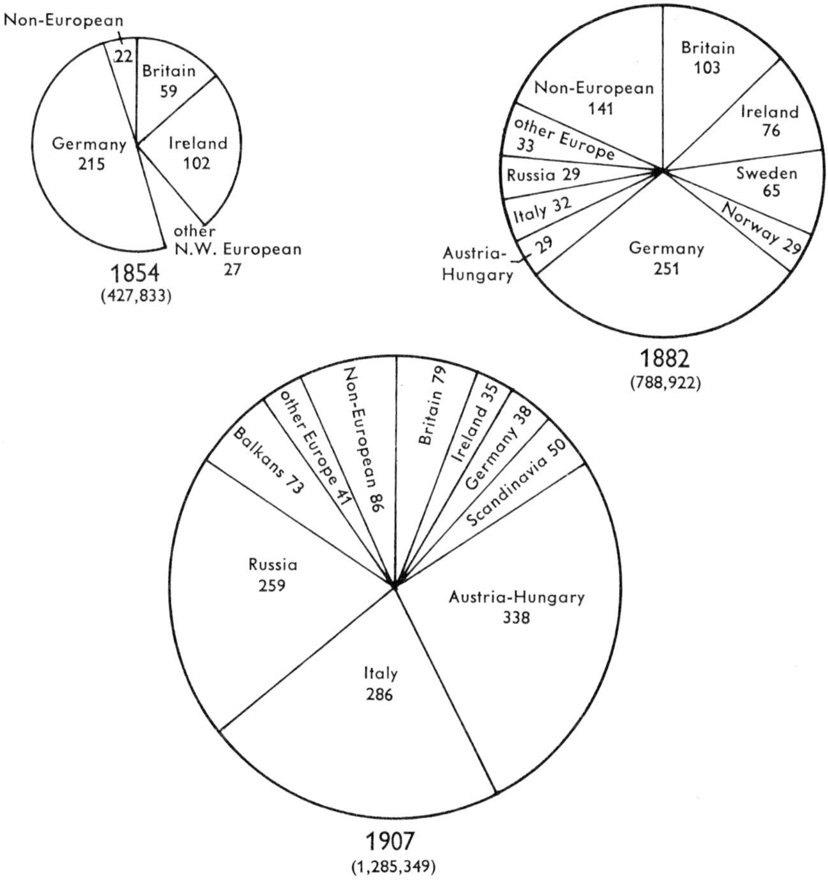

American immigration:
three peak years
(figures within circles in 000's)

There is one other way in which the foreign elements might amalgamate with each other and with the native, so as in the course of time to form one homogeneous people, – that is by intermarriage. In the case of the blacks there is the insuperable color obstacle in the way of their fusion with the whites. But in the case of the immigrants this does not exist, and the impediments of difference in language, customs, and even religion may gradually be removed. It is a question of great interest how far such a fusion of blood is actually occurring in the United States.

The statistics on this point are not very encouraging to those persons who believe that mixture of blood in the United States will finally produce a race different from and superior to any of the older nationalities. It appears that where a particular nationality is concentrated in any one locality, the men choose wives of their own race. . . .

It is possible that the future generations of different blood may intermarry more freely. But even here it is seen how desirable it is to break up the concentration of immigrants of the same nationality in one place, so that by intermarriage with the natives and with people of other nationality this process of fusion and amalgamation may be hastened.

It is one of the favorite theories of social philosophers that mixed races are the strongest. And it is true as a matter of history that the most progressive peoples of Europe are mixed in blood. The American people of the future will be a race composed of many different elements, and it is possible that this mixture will have produced a people possessing the best characteristics displayed by these various elements. It seems, however, that there are two things that ought to be carefully considered. One is that the constituent elements of this amalgamation should themselves be of desirable quality. It is scarcely probable that by taking the dregs of Europe we shall produce a people of high social intelligence and morality. The second is that we must see to it that the opportunity for amalgamation is really given. Simply placing these discordant elements in juxtaposition will not make a compact and solid whole. On the contrary it will give rise to an atomistic weakness which will make any homogeneous and harmonious development impossible. A nation is great, not on account of the number of individuals contained within its boundaries, but through the strength begotten of common national ideals and aspirations. No nation can exist and be powerful that is not homogeneous in this sense. And the great ethnic problem we have before us is to fuse these diverse elements into one common nationality, having one language, one political practice, one patriotism and one ideal of social development.

---

104 **amalgamate** (v.): mix 106 *intermarriage* (n.): marriage between members of different nationalities, ethnic minorities, etc. 106 *insuperable* (adj.): (of difficulties, etc.) that cannot be overcome 107 **obstacle** (n.): s. th. in the way that stops progress or makes it difficult 108 *impediment* (n.): s. th. that hinders, esp. a defect in speech 127 *constituent* (adj.) /kən`stɪtʃʊənt/: forming or helping to make a whole; component part 128 *dregs* (pl. n.): worst and useless part 131 *discordant* (adj.): not in agreement 131 *juxtaposition* (n.): placing side by side 131 *compact* (adj.) /kəm`pækt/: neatly fitted 132 *atomistic* (adj.): made up of a number of unrelated elements 135 **aspiration** (n.): desire.

8: ISRAEL ZANGWILL: America is God's Crucible*

Israel Zangwill (1864–1926), an English Jewish writer and a Zionist, wrote a great number of novels and plays about Jews in the diaspora. His play *The Melting-Pot* (1909) was dedicated to Theodore Roosevelt, who was President of the United States from 1901–1909.

The following text is taken from Israel Zangwill, *The Melting-Pot;* in *Works of Israel Zangwill: The Melting-Pot; Chosen Peoples* (New York: The American Jewish Book Company, 1921), pp. 33, 95–98.

[The main character in the play, David, a Jew who was born in Kishineff (then in Russian Bessarabia) and now lives in New York, says]

"America is God's crucible, the great Melting Pot, where all the races of Europe are re-forming. Here you stand, good folk, think I, when I see them at Ellis Island, here you stand in your fifty groups with your fifty languages and histories and your fifty bloodhatreds and rivalries. But you won't long be like that, brothers, for these are the fires of God you've come to – these are the fires of God. A fig for your feuds and vendettas. Germans and Frenchmen, Irishmen and Englishmen, Jews and Russians, into the crucible with you all. God is making the American."

[The following dialogue stands in this context: David most clearly advocates rejecting Judaism during an argument about his engagement to Vera Revendal, a Russian Christian noblewomen. David tells his uncle Mendel the news, and Mendel replies that the lovers cannot marry]

(Title) **crucible** (n.): pot in which metals are melted; Schmelztiegel.

(Introduction) 1 *Zionist* (n.) /ˈzaɪənɪst/: supporter of a political movement for the establishment of an independent state for the Jews 2 *diaspora* (n.) /daɪˈæspərə/: the dispersion (Zerstreuung) of the Jews among the Gentiles (Nichtjuden) after their period of exile 3 **dedicate** (v.): (of an author) write or print a person's name at the beginning of a book (to show gratitude or friendship to); widmen.

2 *re-form* (v.): form again; neugestalten 2 *good folk* (n.): good people 2 *Ellis Island* (n.): island southwest of Manhatten; the United States' chief immigration station from 1892 to 1943 4 *rivalry* (n.) /ˈraɪvlrɪ/: competition 5 *fig:* give a fig for = not care in the least 5 *feud* (n.) /fjud/: bitter quarrel between two persons, families or groups, over a long period of time 6 *vendetta* (n.): hereditary feud (Erbfehde) between families in which members of each family commit murders in revenge for previous murders.

(Context) 1 **advocate** (v.): support 2 *engagement* (n.): agreement to marry.

David. *You* say that! You who have come to the heart of the Crucible where the roaring fires of God are fusing our race with all the others.

Mendel. Not *our* race, not your race and mine.

David. What immunity has our race? The pride and the prejudice, the dreams and the sacrifices, the traditions and the superstitions, the fasts and the feasts, things noble and things sordid – they must all into the Crucible.

Mendel. The Jew has been tried in a thousand fires and only tempered and annealed.

David. Fires of hate, not fires of love. This is what melts.

Mendel. So I see.

David. Your sneer is false. The love that melted me was not Vera's – it was the love *America* showed me – the day she gathered me to her breast.

Mendel. Many countries have gathered us. Holland took us when we were driven from Spain – but we did not become Dutchmen. Turkey took us when Germany oppressed us, but we have not become Turks.

David. These countries were not in the making. They were old civilizations stamped with the seal of greed. In such countries the Jew may be right or stand out. But here in this new secular Republic we must look forward –

Mendel. We must look backwards, too.

David. To what? To Kishineff? To that butcher's face directing the slaughter? To those –?

Mendel. Hush! Calm yourself!

David. Yes, I will calm myself – but how else shall I calm myself save by forgetting all that nightmare of religions and races, save by holding out my hands with prayer and music toward the Republic of Man and the Kingdom of God! The past I cannot mend – its evil outlines are stamped in immortal rigidity. Take away the hope that I can mend the future and you make me mad.

Mendel. You are mad already – your dreams are mad – the Jew is hated here as everywhere – you are false to your race.

David. I keep faith with America. I have faith America will keep faith with me. *[He raises his hands in religious rapture toward the flag over the door.]*

---

9 **fuse** (v.): join, become joined, as the result of melting 11 *immunity* (n.): freedom from an obligation 11 **prejudice** (n.) /ˈpredʒədɪs/: opinion, like or dislike, formed before one has adequate knowledge or experience 12 *superstition* (n.): (idea, practice, etc. founded on) unreasoning belief in magic, witchcraft, etc.; Aberglaube 12 *fast* (n.): (period of) going without food 13 *sordid* (adj.): wretched; contemptible 14 *try* (v.): extract or refine (metal, etc.) by heating 14 *temper* (v.): give the required degree of toughness to steel by heating and cooling 14/15 *anneal* (v.): cool (metals, glass, etc.) very slowly after heating, in order to toughen and temper 18 **sneer** (n.): contemptuous smile or utterance 22 **oppress** (v.): keep down by unjust or cruel government; unterdrücken 23 *in the making*: in a stage of development 24 **greed** (n.): strong desire for more than is right or reasonable; Habgier 25 *secular* (adj.) /ˈsekjʊlə(r)/: worldly, not religious or spiritual 32 **nightmare** (n.): terrible, frightening dream; Alptraum 34 **outline** (n.): line(s) showing shape or boundary 35 *rigidity* (n.): inflexibility.

9: HORACE M. KALLEN: Democracy versus the Melting Pot*

The proponents of cultural pluralism were unwilling to accept the assumption, implicit in the melting pot idea, that all the peoples who came to the United States would ultimately fuse in a homogeneous mass. In an influential series of articles in 1915, the philosopher Horace M. Kallen set forth the thesis that American society constituted a federation of cultures. He denied that it was possible or desirable for the immigrant groups to lose their identity and argued that American culture had much to gain by permitting each of them to develop its own particular tendencies.

The following article first appeared in *The Nation,* 100 (1915), 219–220 and is taken from Oscar Handlin, ed., *Immigration as a Factor in American History* (Englewood Cliffs, N. J.: Prentice-Hall, 1959), pp. 153–155.

We are, in fact, at the parting of the ways. A genuine social alternative is before us, either of which parts we may realize if we will. . . . What do we will to make of the United States – a unison, singing the old Anglo-Saxon theme "America", the America of the New England school, or a harmony, in which that theme shall be dominant, perhaps, among others, but one among many, not the only one? . . .

The attainment of . . . a harmony . . . requires concerted public action. But the action . . . would seek simply to eliminate the waste and the stupidity of our social organization, by way of freeing and strengthening the strong forces actually in operation. Starting with our existing ethnic and cultural groups, it would seek to provide conditions under which each may attain the perfection that is proper to its kind. The provision of such conditions is the primary intent of our fundamental law and the function of our institutions. And the various nationalities which compose our commonwealth must learn first of all this fact, which is perhaps, to most minds, the outstanding ideal content of "Americanism" – that democracy means self-realization through self-control, self-government, and that one is impossible without the other. . . .

(Title) *versus* (prep.) /ˋvɛsəs/: against.

(Introduction) 1 **proponent** (n.) /prəˋpəʊnənt/: one who supports a cause 1 *assumption* (n.): s. th. taken for granted 2 **implicit** (pred. adj.) /ɪmˋplɪsɪt/: implied though not plainly expressed 3 *ultimately* (adv.): finally 3 **fuse** (v.): join, become joined, as the result of melting 3 **homogeneous** (adj.) /ˈhəʊməˋdʒinɪəs/: (formed of parts) of the same kind 5 **federation** (n.): politischer Bund.

3 *unison* (n.) /ˋjunɪsn̩/: concord or agreement 6 *attainment* (n.): accomplishment 6 *concert* (v.): arrange with others; plan 7 *eliminate* (v.): take or put away 9 **ethnic** (adj.): of race or nation; of a minority or nationality group that is part of a larger community 11 *provision* (n.): a providing or preparing 11 *intent* (n.): (chiefly legal) purpose.

What is inalienable in the life of mankind is its intrinsic positive quality – its psychophysical inheritance. Men may change their clothes, their politics, their wives, their religions, their philosophies, to a greater or lesser extent: they cannot change their grandfathers. Jews or Poles or Anglo-Saxons, in order to cease being Jews or Poles or Anglo-Saxons, would have to cease to be. The selfhood which is inalienable in them, and for the realization of which they require "inalienable" liberty, is ancestrally determined, and the happiness which they pursue has its form implied in ancestral endowment. This is what, actually, democracy in operation assumes. There are human capacities which it is the function of the state to liberate and to protect; and the failure of the state as a government means its abolition. . . . As intelligence and wisdom prevail over "politics" and special interests, as the steady and continuous pressure of the inalienable qualities and purposes of human groups more and more dominate the confusion of our common life, the outlines of a possible great and truly democratic commonwealth become discernible.

Its form is that of the Federal republic; its substance a democracy of nationalities, co-operating voluntarily and autonomously in the enterprise of self-realization through the perfection of men according to their kind. The common language of the commonwealth, the language of its great political tradition, is English, but each nationality expresses its emotional and voluntary life in its own language, in its own inevitable aesthetic and intellectual forms. The common life of the commonwealth is politico-economic, and serves as the foundation and background for the realization of the distinctive individuality of each *natio* that composes it. Thus "American civilization" may come to mean the perfection of the cooperative harmonies of "European civilization", the waste, the squalor, and the distress of Europe being eliminated – a multiplicity in a unity, an orchestration of mankind. As in an orchestra,

---

17 **inalienable** (adj.) /ɪn`eɪlɪənəbl/: of rights that cannot be given away or taken away; unveräußerlich 17 *intrinsic* (adj.): belonging naturally; existing within, not without 18 *psychophysical* (adj.) /'saɪkəʊ`fɪzɪkl/: psychophysisch 18 **inheritance** (b.): the deriving of qualities from ancestors; Erbschaft 21 *selfhood* (n.): all the things that make a person what he is; personality or individuality 24 **ancestral** (adj.) /æn`sestrl/: belonging to, having come from one's ancestors (Vorfahren) 24 *endowment* (n.) /ɪn`daʊmənt/: possession of qualities that one is born with 26 *abolition* (n.): doing away with; Abschaffung 29 **outline** (n.): line(s) showing shape or boundary; Kontur, Umriß 30 *commonwealth* (n.): politisches Gemeinwesen 30 *discernible* (adj.): that can be seen clearly 32 *co-operate* (v.): work or act together in order to bring about a result 32 **voluntary** (adj.) /`volənterɪ/: ready to do things without being compelled 32 *autonomous* (adj.) /ɔ`tonəməs/: autonom 32 **enterprise** (n.): undertaking 36 **inevitable** (adj.) /ɪn`evɪtəbl/: that cannot be avoided; unvermeidlich 36 **aesthetic** (adj.) /'ɪs`θetɪk/: of the appreciation of the beautiful, esp. in the arts 36 **intellectual** (adj.) /'ɪntə`lektʃʊəl/: of the intellect 38 *distinctive* (adj.) serving to mark a difference 38 *individuality* (n.) /'ɪndɪ`vɪdʒʊ`ælətɪ/: Individualität 38 *natio* (n.): Latin for nation 40 **squalor** (n.) /`skwolə(r)/: filth and wretchedness 41 *orchestration* (n.): composing, arranging, scoring for orchestral performances 41 *orchestra* (n.) /`ɔkɪstrə/: Orchester.

every type of instrument has its specific timbre and tonality, founded in its substance and form; as every type has its appropriate theme and melody in the whole symphony, so in society each ethnic group is the natural instrument, its spirit and culture are its theme and melody, and the harmony and dissonances and discords of them all make the symphony of civilization, with this difference: a musical symphony is written before it is played; in the symphony of civilization the playing is the writing, so that there is nothing so fixed and inevitable about its progressions as in music, so that within the limits set by nature they may vary at will, and the range and variety of the harmonies may become wider and richer and more beautiful.

But the question is, do the dominant classes in America want such a society?

"Chewing the food of sweet and bitter fancy."
Immigrants at Ellis Island dreaming of *spaghetti, gefillte fish,* and *Schweinebraten mit Sauerkraut.*

---

42 *timbre* (n.): /tæ̃br/: characteristic quality of sound 42 *tonality* (n.): character of a melody 43 **appropriate** (adj.): fitting; passend; angemessen 45 *dissonance* (n.): Dissonanz 45 *discord* (n.): lack of harmony between sounds 48 **progression** (n.): progress; moving forward.

10: ROBERT HAVEN SCHAUFFLER: Scum o' the Earth

Robert Haven Schauffler (1879–1953) was an American poet, essayist, musical biographer, and anthologist. The following poem was first collected in *Scum o' the Earth and Other Poems* (1912).

This text is taken from Max J. Herzberg, ed., *This Is America* (New York: Pocket Books, 1950), pp. 75–78.

– I –

At the gate of the West I stand,
On the island where nations throng.
We call them "scum o' the earth";

Stay, are we doing you wrong,
Young fellow from Socrates' land? –
You, like a Hermes so lithe and strong
Fresh from the master Praxiteles' hand?
So you're of Spartan birth?
Descended, perhaps, from one of the band –
Deathless in story and song –
Who combed their long hair at Thermopylae's pass? . . .
Ah, I forget what straits, (alas!),
More tragic than theirs, more compassion-worth,
Have doomed you to march in our "immigrant class"
Where you're nothing but "scum o' the earth."

(Introduction) 2 *anthologist* (n.): person who collects and edits poems, or pieces of prose by one writer or different writers.

2 *throng* (v.): crowd 6 *lithe* (adj.) /laɪð/: (of a person, a body) bending, twisting or turning easily 9 **descend from** (v.): abstammen von 13 *compassion* (n.): pity 14 *doom* (v.): condemn.

– II –

You Pole with the child on your knee,
What dower have you to the land of the free?
Hark! does she croon
The sad little tune
Chopin once mined from the Polish air
And mounted in gold for us to wear?
Now a ragged young fiddler answers
In wild Czech melody
That Dvorák took whole from the dancers.
And the heavy faces bloom
In the wonderful Slavic way;
The dull little eyes, the foreheads' gloom,
Are suddenly fair and gay,
While, watching these folk and their mystery,
I forget that we,
In our scornful mirth,
Brand them as "polacks" – and "scum o' the earth."

– III –

Genoese boy of the level brow,
Lad of the lustrous, dreamy eyes
Agaze at Manhattan's pinnacles now
In the first, glad shock of a hushed surprise;
Within your far-rapt seer's eyes
I catch the glow of the wild surmise
That played on the *Santa Maria's* prow
In that still gray dawn,
Four centuries gone,
When a world from the wave began to rise.

---

17 *dower* (n.) /ˈdaʊə(r)/: (arch.) gift by a man to his bride 18 *hark* (v.): (chiefly used as an imperative) listen 18 *croon* (v.): hum or sing gently 20 *mine* (v.): obtain from mines 21 *mount* (v.): fix a jewel, picture, etc., on or in the proper support, backing, setting, etc. 22 *ragged* (adj.) /ˈrægɪd/: badly torn or in rags; zerlumpt 22 *fiddler* (n.): person who plays the fiddle (Violine) 31 *scornful* (adj.): showing or feeling contempt 31 *mirth* (n.): being merry and happy 32 *brand* (v.): brandmarken 32 *polack* (n.): (derog.) person of Polish descent (Abstammung) 33 *Genoese* (adj.) /ˈdʒenʊˈiz/: aus Genua 33 *brow* (n.) /braʊ/: forehead 34 *lustrous* (adj.): having a smooth and bright surface 35 *agaze* (adv.): gazing 35 *pinnacle* (n.): tall, pointed ornament built on to a roof 36 *hush* (v.): make or become silent or quiet 37 *rapt* (adj.): so deep in thought, so carried away by feelings, that one is unaware of other things 37 *seer* (n.): prophet; Seher 38 *surmise* (n.): Vermutung 39 *Santa Maria* (n.): name of the flagship that Columbus used in his voyage of 1492 39 *prow* (n.) /praʊ/: pointed front of a ship.

Oh, who shall foretell what high emprise
Is the goal that gleams
When Italy's dreams
Spread wing and sweep into the skies?
Caesar dreamed him a world ruled well;
Dante dreamed Heaven out of Hell;
Angelo brought us there to dwell;
And you, are you of a different birth? –
You're only a "dago," – "scum o' the earth"!

– IV –

Stay, are we doing you wrong
Calling you "scum o' the earth",
Man of the sorrow-bowed head,
Of the features tender yet strong, –
Man of the eyes full of wisdom and mystery
Mingled with patience and dread?
Have not I known you in history,
Sorrow-bowed head?
Were you the poet-king, worth
Treasures of Ophir unpriced?
Or were you the prophet, whose art
Foretold how the rabble would mock
That shepherd of spirits, erelong,
Who should gather the lambs to his heart
And tenderly feed his flock?
Man – lift that sorrow-bowed head. . . .
Behold, the face of the Christ!

The vision dies at its birth.
You're merely a butt for our mirth.
You're a "sheeny" – and therefore despised
And rejected as "scum o' the earth."

---

43 *foretell* (n.): tell beforehand; predict 43 *emprise* (n.): enterprise or adventure 44 **goal** (n.): object of efforts or ambition 46 *sweep* (v.): move along lightly and quickly 51 *dago* (n.) /ˈdeɪgəʊ/: (derog.) person of Italian descent 60/61 the poet-king ... Treasures of Ophir: King Solomon, the poet-king in the Old Testament, whose ships brought home immense riches, esp. gold, from the land of Ophir (probably Arabia or East Africa) 61 *unpriced* (pred. adj.): too valuable to be priced (mit Geldwert versehen) 63 *rabble* (n.): disorderly crowd; mob 64 *erelong* (adv.) /ˈɪə(r)lɔŋ/: (arch. or poet.) before long; soon 70 **butt** (n.): person who is a target for ridicule, jokes, etc.; Zielscheibe 71 *sheeny* (n.): (derog.) Jew 72 **reject** (v.): abweisen; ablehnen.

One-time immigrants reject new arrival.

– V –

Countrymen, bend and invoke
Mercy for us blasphemers,
For that we spat on these marvelous folk,
Nations of darers and dreamers,
Scions of singers and seers,
Our peers, and more than our peers.
"Rabble and refuse", we name them
And "scum o' the earth", to shame them.
Mercy for us of the few, young years,
Of the culture so callow and crude,
Of the hands so grasping and rude,
The lips so ready for sneers

73 *invoke* (v.): call upon God for help or protection 74 *blasphemer* (n.): /ˋblæsfəmə(r)/: person who speaks in an irreverent (unehrerbietig) way about God and sacred things 77 *scion* (n.) /ˋsɑɪən/: Sproß, Abkömmling 85 *peer* (n.): equal in rank, merit or quality 82 *callow* (adj.): young; inexperienced 82 **crude** (adj.): not having grace, taste or refinement 84 **sneer** (n.): contemptuous look, smile, or word of utterance.

At the sons of our ancient more-than-peers.
Mercy for us who dare despise
Men in whose loins our Homer lies;
Mothers of men who shall bring to us
The glory of Titian, the grandeur of Huss;
Children in whose frail arms may rest
Prophets and singers and saints of the West.

Newcomers all from the eastern seas,
Help us incarnate dreams like these.
Forgive and forget that we did you wrong.
Help us to father a nation strong
In the comradeship of an equal birth,
In the wealth of the richest bloods of earth.

---

87 *loin* (n.): Lende 89 *grandeur* (n.) /ˈgrændʒə(r)/: greatness; magnificence 90 *frail* (adj.): weak; fragile 93 *incarnate* (v.) /ɪnˈkɑrneit/: put (an idea, etc.) into real or material form 95 *father* (v.): be the originator of.

European immigrants arrive at Ellis Island, which was opened as a receiving station for immigrants in 1892.

11: ANONYMOUS POLISH IMMIGRANT: Letter to the Massachusetts Commission on Immigration

A Polish immigrant wrote the following letter to the Massachusetts Commission on Immigration in August 1914. It was first published in *Report of the Commission on the Problem of Immigration in Massachusetts* (Boston, 1914), p. 134.

This text is from Oscar Handlin, ed., *Immigration as a Factor in American History* (Englewood Cliffs, N. J.: Prentice-Hall, 1959), pp. 163–64.

I'm in this country four months (from 14 Mai 1914 – Noniton – Antverpen).

I am polish man. I want be american citizen – and took here first paper in 12 June N 625. But my friends are polish people – I must live with them – I work in the shoes-shop with polish people – I stay all the time with them – at home – in the shop – anywhere.

I want live with american people, but I do not know anybody of american. I go 4 times to teacher and must pay $ 2 weekly. I wanted take board in english house, but I could not, for I earn only $ 5 or 6 in a week, and when I pay teacher $ 2, I have only $ 2 – $ 3 – and now english board house is too dear for me. Better job to get is very hard for me, because I do not speak well english and I cannot understand what they say to me. The teacher teach me – but when I come home – I must speak polish and in the shop also. In this way I can live in your country many years – like my friends – and never speak – write well english – and never be good american citizen. I know here many persons, they live here 10 or moore years, and they are not citizens, they don't speak well english, they don't know geography and history of this country, they don't know constitution of America – nothing. I don't like be like them I wanted they help me in english – they could not – because they knew nothing. I want go from them away. But where? Not in the country, because I want go in the city, free evening schools and lern. I'm looking for help. If somebody could give me another job between american people, help me live with them and lern english – and could tell me the best way how I can fast lern – it would be very, very good for me. Perhaps you have somebody, here he could help me?

If you can help me, I please you.

I wrote this letter by myself and I know no good – but I hope you will understand whate I mean.

Excuse me,
F. N.

(Title) *anonymous* (adj.) /əˈnɒnɪməs/: without a name; anonym **immigrant** (n.): person who comes as a settler into another country *commission* (n.): body of persons given the duty of making an inquiry (Untersuchung) and writing a report.

7 *board* (n.): meals supplied for payment by the week or month 16 **constitution** (n.): (legal use) laws and principles according to which a state is governed; Verfassung.

12: JOHN F. KENNEDY: Why They Came

John F. Kennedy (1917–1963), President of the United States (1961–63), had a special concern for immigration legislation.

The following text is a chapter from his *A Nation of Immigrants* (New York: Harper and Row, 1964), pp. 4–9.

Little is more extraordinary than the decision to migrate, little more extraordinary than the accumulation of emotions and thoughts which finally leads a family to say farewell to a community where it has lived for centuries, to abandon old ties and familiar landmarks, and to sail across dark seas to a strange land. Today, when mass communications tell one part of the world all about another, it is relatively easy to understand how poverty or tyranny might compel people to exchange an old nation for a new one. But centuries ago migration was a leap into the unknown. It was an enormous intellectual and emotional commitment. The forces that moved our forebears to their great decision – the decision to leave their homes and begin an adventure filled with incalculable uncertainty, risk and hardship – must have been of overpowering proportions.

Oscar Handlin, in his book *The Uprooted,* describes the experience of the immigrants:

"The crossing immediately subjected the emigrant to a succession of shattering shocks and decisively conditioned the life of every man that survived it. This was the initial contact with life as it was to be. For many peasants it was the first time away

---

(Introduction) 2 **concern** (n.): interest in or regard for a person or thing 2 **immigration legislation** (n.): making laws concerning persons who come as settlers into another country.

1 **migrate** (v.) /ˋmaɪgreɪt/: move from one place to another to live there 2 **accumulation** (n.): making or becoming greater in number or quantity 3 *abandon* (v.) /əˋbændən/: go away from 4 *landmark* (n.): prominent feature of the landscape, distinguishing a locality 8 **commitment** (n.): binding as by a promise 9 **forebears** (usually pl. n.): ancestors; Vorfahren 10 *incalculable* (adj.): that cannot be reckoned beforehand 10 **hardship** (n.): circumstance that causes discomfort or suffering 11 *overpowering* (adj.): too strong, overwhelming 13 **immigrant** (n.): person who comes as a settler into another country 14 *subject* (v.): expose 14 **emigrant** (n.): person who goes away from his own country to another to settle there 14 *succession* (n.): the coming of one thing after another in time or order 14 *shatter* (v.): damage 15 *decisively* (adv.): definitely 15 **condition** (v.): determine 15 **survive** (v.): remain alive after 16 **initial** (adj.) /ɪˋnɪʃl/: of or at the beginning.

from home, away from the safety of the circumscribed little villages in which they had passed all their years. Now they would learn to have dealings with people essentially different from themselves. Now they would collide with unaccustomed problems, learn to understand alien ways and alien languages, manage to survive in a grossly foreign environment."

Initially, they had to save up money for passage. Then they had to say good-bye to cherished relatives and friends, whom they could expect never to see again. They started their journey by traveling from their villages to the ports of embarkation. Some walked; the luckier trundled their few possessions into carts which they sold before boarding ship. Some paused along the road to work in the fields in order to eat. Before they even reached the ports of embarkation, they were subject to illness, accidents, storm and snow, even to attacks by outlaws.

After arriving at the ports, they often had to wait days, weeks, sometimes months, while they bargained with captains or agents for passage. Meanwhile, they crowded into cheap lodginghouses near the quays, sleeping on straw in small, dark rooms, sometimes as many as forty in a room twelve by fifteen feet.

Until the middle of the nineteenth century the immigrants traveled in sailing vessels. The average trip from Liverpool to New York took forty days; but any estimate of time was hazardous, for the ship was subject to winds, tides, primitive navigation, unskilled seamanship and the whim of the captain. A good size for the tiny craft of those days was three hundred tons, and each one was crowded with anywhere from four hundred to a thousand passengers.

For the immigrants, their shipboard world was the steerage, that confined space below deck, usually about seventy-five feet long and twenty-five feet wide. In many vessels no one over five and a half feet tall could stand upright. Here they lived their days and nights, receiving their daily ration of vinegar-flavored water and trying to eke out sustenance from whatever provisions they had brought along. When their

---

17 *circumscribe* (v.): confine 18 *dealings* (pl. n.): relations 19 **collide** (v.): come into violent contact 19 *unaccustomed* (adj.): not accustomed (to) 20 **alien** (adj.) /ˋeɪlɪən/: foreign 20 *gross* (adj.) /grəʊs/: entire 21 **environment** (n.) /ɪnˋvɑɪərnmənt/: surroundings, circumstances, influences; Milieu 23 *cherish* (v.): care for tenderly 24 **embarkation** (n.): going on board a ship 25 *trundle* (v.): (esp. of s. th. heavy or awkward in shape) move or roll 26 **board** (v.): get on a ship 26 *pause* (v.) make a short interval or stop 28 *outlaw* (n.): criminal 30 *bargain* (v.) /ˋbɑgɪn/: talk for the purpose of reaching an agreement about buying or selling s. th.; aushandeln, feilschen 31 *lodginghouse* (n.): house in which rooms are let 31 *quay* (n.) /ki/: solid stationary landing-place, alongside which ships can be tied up; Kai 35 *hazardous* (adj.) /ˋhæzədəs/: risky 36 *navigation* (n.): art or science of plotting the course, finding the position, etc. of a ship using charts and instruments 36 **unskilled** (adj.): (of workers) not having special skill or special training 36 *seamanship* (n.): skill in managing a boat or ship 39 **steerage** (n.): that part of a ship nearest the rudder; this section formerly used for providing for passengers travelling at the lowest fares 42 *ration* (n.) /ˋræʃn/: fixed quantity, esp. of food, allowed to one person 42 *vinegar* (n.) /ˋvɪnɪgə(r)/: Essig 42 *flavor* (v.): (AE spelling for BE flavour) give a distinctive taste to 43 *eke out* (v.) /ik/: manage to make a living with difficulty 43 *sustenance* (n.) /ˋsʌstɪnəns/: (nourishing quality of) food or drink 43 **provisions** (pl. n.): food supplies.

food ran out, they were often at the mercy of extortionate captains.

They huddled in their hard, cramped bunks, freezing when the hatches were open, stifling when they were closed. The only light came from a dim, swaying lantern. Night and day were indistinguishable. But they were ever aware of the treacherous winds and waves, the scampering of rats and the splash of burials. Diseases – cholera, yellow fever, smallpox and dysentery – took their toll. One in ten failed to survive the crossing.

Eventually the journey came to an end. The travelers saw the coast of America with mixed feelings of relief, excitement, trepidation and anxiety. For now, uprooted from old patterns of life, they found themselves, in Handlin's phrase, "in a prolonged state of crisis – crisis in the sense that they were, and remained, unsettled." They reached the new land exhausted by lack of rest, bad food, confinement and the strain of adjustment to new conditions. But they could not pause to recover their strength. They had no reserves of food or money; they had to keep moving until they found work. This meant new strains at a time when their capacity to cope with new problems had already been overburdened.

There were probably as many reasons for coming to America as there were people who came. It was a highly individual decision. Yet it can be said that three large forces – religious persecution, political oppression and economic hardship – provided the chief motives for the mass migrations to our shores. They were responding, in their own way, to the pledge of the Declaration of Independence: the promise of "life, liberty and the pursuit of happiness."

The search for freedom of worship has brought people to America from the days of the Pilgrims to modern times. In our own day, for example, anti-Semitic and anti-Christian persecution in Hitler's Germany and the Communist empire have driven people from their homes to seek refuge in America. Not all found what they sought

---

44 *extortionate* (adj.) /ɪk`stɔʃnət/: in the nature of extortion (= getting money from s. b. by force or threats) 45 **huddle** (v.): crowd together 45 *cramp* (v.): restrain; hinder or prevent the movement of 45 *bunk* (n.): bed fixed on the wall of a cabin in a ship 45 *hatch* (n.): movable covering over an opening in a door or floor, esp. one in a ship's deck through which cargo is lowered and raised 46 *stifle* (v.) /`staɪfl/: give or have the feeling that breathing is difficult 46 *sway* (v.): move first to on side and then to the other 47 *treacherous* (adj.) /`tretʃərəs/: untrustworthy, not to be relied upon 48 *scamper* (v.): (esp. of small animals) run quickly 48 *splash* (n.): sound made by splashing (= aufklatschen) 48 *burial* (n.) /`berɪəl/: burying; Begräbnis 49 *smallpox* (n.): serious contagious (= ansteckend) disease which leaves permanent marks on the skin 49 *dysentery* (n.) /`dɪsntərɪ/: painful disease of the bowels with discharge of mucus and blood; Ruhr 49 *toll* (n.): s. th. paid, lost or suffered; Zoll 52 *trepidation* (n.): excited state of mind 52 **anxiety** (n.) /æŋg`zaɪətɪ/: Angst 53 *Handlin*: reference to Oscar Handlin, *The Uprooted* (Boston, 1951). Handlin, an American historian, describes in a vivid manner the experience of the immigrant during his passage from the Old World to the New World. 53 *prolonged* (adj.): continuing for a long time 56 **adjustment** (n.): Anpassung 56 *recover* (v.): get back to a former state of health 58 **cope with** (v.): manage successfully 59 *overburden* (v.): burden too heavily 62 **persecution** (n.): treating or having treated cruelly, esp. because of religious belief 62 **oppression** (n.): condition of being kept down by unjust or cruel government 64 *pledge* (n.): promise 67 **Pilgrims:** cf. explanation of "the western pilgrims" in text 2, line 90.

immediately. The Puritans of the Massachusetts Bay Colony, who drove Roger Williams and Anne Hutchinson into the wilderness, showed as little tolerance for dissenting beliefs as the Anglicans of England had shown to them. Minority religious sects, from the Quakers and Shakers through the Catholics and Jews to the Mormons and Jehovah's Witnesses, have at various times suffered both discrimination and hostility in the United States.

But the very diversity of religious belief has made for religious toleration. In demanding freedom for itself, each sect had increasingly to permit freedom for others. The insistence of each successive wave of immigrants upon its right to practice its religion helped make freedom of worship a central part of the American creed. People who gambled their lives on the right to believe in their own God would not lightly surrender that right in a new society.

The second great force behind immigration has been political oppression. America has always been a refuge from tyranny. As a nation conceived in liberty, it has held out to the world the promise of respect for the rights of man. Every time a revolution has failed in Europe, every time a nation has succumbed to tyranny, men and women who love freedom have assembled their families and their belongings and set sail across the seas. Nor has this process come to an end in our own day. The Russian Revolution, the terrors of Hitler's Germany and Mussolini's Italy, the Communist suppression of the Hungarian Revolution of 1956, and the cruel measures of the Castro regime in Cuba – all have brought new thousands seeking sanctuary in the United States.

---

70 **the Puritans of the Massachusetts Bay Colony:** the Puritans who came to Massachusetts (*Mayflower,* 1620) in the 17th century established their social ideal of a theocracy, with powerful ministers and absolute control of individual conduct. The family was the fortress of godliness, and life was to be lived in strict obedience to detailed laws of God as read in the Bible. The Massachusetts Bay Colony was until 1684 synonymous with the Massachusetts Bay Company, an English chartered company, organized in 1628 with a grant of land between the Charles and Merrimac rivers, extending West to "the South Sea". 70/71 *Roger Williams*: clergyman, advocate of religious freedom, was banished from Massachusetts and founded Providence, Rhode Island, in 1636. 71 *Anne Hutchinson*: religious leader in New England, was banished from Massachusetts Bay Colony as an antinomian heretic. She and her followers founded Portsmouth, Rhode Island, in 1638.

71 **tolerance** (n.): quality of tolerating opinions, beliefs, customs, behaviour, etc. different from one's own 72 *dissent* (v.): have a different opinion from 72 *Anglican* (n.): member of the Church of England 72 **minority** (n. and adj.) /maɪˋnorətɪ; AE məˋnorətɪ/: a racial, religious or political group that differs from the larger, controlling group 73 *sect* (n.): group of people united by religious beliefs or opinions that differ from those more generally accepted 74 **discrimination** (n.): showing partiality or prejudice; Diskriminierung 75 **hostility** (n.): enmity; ill will 76 **diversity** (n.) /ˈdɑɪˋvɛsətɪ; AE ˈdəˋvɛsɪtɪ/: variety 76 *make for* (v.): move in the direction of 78 *insistence* (n.): insisting or being insisted 79 *creed* (n.): (system of) beliefs or opinions, esp. on religious doctrine 80 *gamble* (v.): take great risks for the chance of winning s. th. 83 **tyranny** (n.) /ˋtɪrənɪ/: cruel and unjust use of power 85 *succumb* (v.) /səˋkʌm/: yield; give way (to) 89 *measure* (n.): course of action 90 *sanctuary* (n.) /ˋsæŋktʃʊərɪ/: place of refuge.

The economic factor has been more complex than the religious and political factors. From the very beginning, some have come to America in search of riches, some in flight from poverty and some because they were bought and sold and had no choice. And the various reasons have intertwined. Thus some early arrivals were lured to these shores by dreams of amassing great wealth, like the Spanish conquistadors in Mexico and Peru. These adventurers, expecting quick profits in gold, soon found that real wealth lay in such crops as tobacco and cotton. As they built up the plantation economy in states like Virginia and the Carolinas, they needed cheap labor. So they began to import indentured servants from England, men and women who agreed to labor a term of years in exchange for eventual freedom, and slaves from Africa.

The process of industrialization in America increased the demand for cheap labor, and chaotic economic conditions in Europe increased the supply. If some immigrants continued to believe that the streets of New York were paved with gold, more were driven by the hunger and hardship of their native lands. The Irish potato famine of 1845 brought almost a million people to America in five years. American manufacturers advertised in European newspapers, offering to pay the passage of any man willing to come to America to work for them.

The immigrants who came for economic reasons contributed to the strength of the new society in several ways. Those who came from countries with advanced political and economic institutions brought with them faith in those institutions and experience in making them work. They also brought technical and managerial skills which contributed greatly to economic growth in the new land. Above all, they helped give America the extraordinary social mobility which is the essence of an open society. In the community he had left, the immigrant usually had a fixed place. He would carry on his father's craft or trade; he would farm his father's land, or that small portion of it that was left to him after it was divided with his brothers. Only with the most exceptional talent and enterprise could he break out of the mold in which life had cast him. There was no such mold for him in the New World. Once having broken with the past, except for sentimental ties and cultural inheritance, he had to rely on his own abilities. It was the future and not the past to which he was compelled to address himself. Except for the Negro slave, he could go anywhere and do anything

---

92 *complex* (adj.): made up of closely connected parts; difficult to understand or explain 94 *intertwine* (v.): become twined or twisted together 95 *lure* (v.) /lʊə(r)/: attract; anlocken 96 *amass* (v.): pile or heap up, collect (esp. riches) 96 *Spanish conquistadors*: the Spaniards who conquered both the Inca empire (Pizarro in 1533) and the Aztec empire (Cortés in 1521); the correct Spanish word for conquerors is *conquistadores*. 100 *indenture* (v.) /ɪnˈdentʃə(r)/: bind a person (esp. a servant or an apprentice) by a written agreement to a master; cf. text 5, intr. l. 8 99 *servant* (n.): person who works in a household for wages, food, and lodging 105 **famine** (n.) /ˈfæmɪn/: extreme scarcity of food in a region; Hungersnot 106/107 **manufacturer** (n.) /ˌmænjʊˈfæktʃə-rə(r)/: owner of a firm that produces goods on a large scale by machinery 112 *managerial* (adj.) /ˌmænɪˈdʒɪərɪəl/: of managers 114 **mobility** (n.): easy change of social status 116 *craft* (n.): occupation, esp. one in which skill in the use of the hands is needed 118 **enterprise** (n.): courage and willingness to engage in undertakings 118 **mold** (n.): (AE spelling for BE mould) pattern, model 120 **inheritance** (n.): receiving s. th. as heir; Erbe 122 *address oneself to* (v.): apply oneself to, be busy with; sich widmen.

"Welcome to all!" *A cartoon from 1880*

his talents permitted. A sprawling continent lay before him, and he had only to weld it together by canals, by railroads and by roads. If he failed to achieve the dream for himself, he could still retain it for his children.

This has been the foundation of American inventiveness and ingenuity, of the multiplicity of new enterprises, and of the success in achieving the highest standard of living anywhere in the world.

These were the major forces that triggered this massive migration. Every immigrant served to reinforce and strengthen those elements in American society that had attracted him in the first place. The motives of some were commonplace. The motives of others were noble. Taken together they add up to the strengths and weaknesses of America.

---

123 *sprawl* (v.): spread out irregularly over much space 123 **weld** (v.): join (pieces of metal) by hammering or pressure (usually when the metal is softened by heat) 126 *inventiveness* (n.): ability to create or design (s. th. not existing before) 126 **ingenuity** (n.) /ˈɪndʒɪˈnjuətɪ/: cleverness and skill 127 *multiplicity* (n.): great number or variety 129 **major** (adj.): greater or more important 129 *trigger* (v.): be the immediate cause of; auslösen 130 **reinforce** (v.): make stronger by adding or supplying more men or material 131 **commonplace** (adj.): ordinary or usual 132 *add up to* (v.): cause an increase to.

The wisest Americans have always understood the significance of the immigrant. Among the "long train of abuses and usurpation" that impelled the framers of the Declaration of Independence to the fateful step of separation was the charge that the British monarch had restricted immigration: "He has endeavoured to prevent the population of these States; for that reason obstructing the Laws for the Naturalization of Foreigners; refusing to pass others to encourage their migrations hither, and raising the conditions of new Appropriations of Lands."

---

134 **significance** (n.): importance 135 *abuse* (n.): mistreatment 135 *usurpation* (n.) /ˈjuzɛˋpeɪʃn/: (instance of) wrongfully taking somebody's power, authority, position, etc. 135 *impel* (v.): drive, force, urge 135 *framer* (n.): constructor; person who plans a theory, a constitution (= Verfassung), etc. 136 *fateful* (adj.): important and decisive 136 *charge* (n.): accusation 137 **restrict** (v.): limit; einschränken 138 **obstruct** (v.): make difficult; hinder 138 **naturalization** (n.) /AE ˈnætʃrlɪˋzeɪʃn; BE –lɑɪˋz–/: Einbürgerung 139 *hither* (adv.) /ˋhɪðə(r)/: (old use) here 140 *appropriation* (n.): Erwerb.

Two Italian Boys Starting out in the New World

13: JOHN F. KENNEDY: The Germans

The following text is a chapter from John F. Kennedy's *A Nation of Immigrants* (New York: Harper and Row, 1964), pp. 51–55.

Between 1830 and 1930, the period of the greatest migration from Europe to the United States, Germany sent six million people to the United States – more than any other nation. Their migrations, increasing in numbers after 1850, overlapped the Irish, whose immigration declined.

The Germans were unique among immigrant groups in their wide dispersal, both geographically and occupationally. This was due, at least in part, to the fact that most of them came with some resources, and were not forced to cluster along the Eastern seaboard. Attracted to the United States by cheap public and railroad lands, and later by free homesteads, the German farmer helped to farm the New West and to cultivate the Mississippi Valley. German artisans, much sought after because of their skills, became an important factor in industrial expansion.

Almost every state in the Union profited from their intellectual and material contributions. Hard-working and knowledgeable about agricultural methods, the Germans became propagators of scientific farming, crop rotation, soil conservation. They share with the Scandinavians the credit for turning millions of acres of wilderness into productive farm land.

The urban settlers lent a distinctive German flavor to many of our cities. Cincinnati, then known as "Queen City" of the West, Baltimore, St. Louis, Minneapolis and Milwaukee, all had substantial German populations. Milwaukee has perhaps retained its distinctive German character longer than any of the others.

In these urban centers Germans entered the fields of education, science, engineering and the arts. German immigrants founded and developed industrial

---

(Introduction) 1 **immigrant** (n.): person who comes as a settler into another country.

1 **migration** (n.) /maɪˈgreɪʃn/: moving from one place to another 3 *overlap* (v.): extend over so as to coincide in part; überlappen 4 **immigration** (n.): coming as a settler into another country 5 **unique** (adj.): having no like or equal 5 *dispersal* (n.): scattering or being scattered 6 **due to:** AE caused by 7 *resources* (pl. n.): wealth 7 *cluster* (v.): form a close group 9 *homestead* (n.): land given to a settler on condition that he lives on it and cultivates it 10 *artisan* (n.): skilled workman in industry and trade 11 *expansion* (n.): making or becoming larger 13 **contribution** (n.): s. th. contributed; Beitrag 13 *knowledgeable* (adj.): well-informed 14 *propagator* (n.): person who spreads ideas, customs, etc. 14 *crop rotation* (n.): varying the crops grown each year on the same land to avoid exhausting the soil 15 *credit* (n.): honour 17 **urban** (adj.): of or in a town 17 *flavor* (n.): (BE spelling flavour) special quality or characteristic 19 **substantial** large; considerable.

German immigrant musicians practice in a park in Madison, Wisconsin (1897).

enterprises in the fields of lumbering, food-processing, brewing, steel-making, electrical engineering, piano-making, railroading and printing.

A small but significant part of the German immigration consisted of political refugees. Reaction in Germany against the reform ideas of the French Revolution had caused heavy suppression of liberal thought. There was strict censorship of the press, of public meetings and of the schools and universities. Nevertheless, a liberal movement had emerged, nurtured in the universities by young intellectuals. This movement led to unsuccessful revolutions in 1830 and 1848. The United States welcomed a large number of veterans of 1848 – men of education, substance and social standing, like Carl Schurz, the statesman and reformer, and General Franz Sigel. In addition, some of the German religious groups established utopian communities in parts of Pennsylvania, Ohio, Indiana, Texas and Oregon.

---

23 **enterprise** (n.): undertaking, esp. one that needs courage or that offers difficulty 23 *lumbering* (n.): cutting down timber (= wood for building houses) and sawing it into lumber (= timber sawed into boards) 23 *food-processing* (n.): putting food through a special process 23 *brewing* (n.): making beer 27 *censorship* (n.): activities of an official with authority to examine newspapers, etc., and to cut out anything undesirable 29 *emerge* (v.): appear; become known 29 *nurture* (v.) /ˈnɜtʃə(r)/: provide with substances necessary to life and growth; promote (= fördern) 33 **utopian** (adj.) /juˈtəʊpɪən/: of a visionary scheme for a perfect society.

German immigration reflected all the chaotic conditions of Central Europe after Napoleon: the population growth, the widespread hunger, the religious dissension and oppression. The Germans included Lutherans, Jews and Catholics, as well as freethinkers. Their talents, training and background greatly enriched the burgeoning nation.

To the influence of the German immigrants in particular – although all minority groups contributed – we owe the mellowing of the austere Puritan imprint on our daily lives. The Puritans observed the Sabbath as a day of silence and solemnity. The Germans clung to their concept of the "Continental Sunday" as a day, not only of churchgoing, but also of relaxation, of picnics, of visiting, of quiet drinking in beer gardens while listening to the music of a band.

The Christmas ritual of religious services combined with exchanging gifts around the Christmas tree is of German origin. So, too, is the celebration of the New Year.

The fact that today almost every large American city has its symphony orchestra can be traced to the influence of the German migration. Leopold Damrosch and his son, Walter, helped build the famous New York Philharmonic. Originally composed mainly of German immigrant musicians and called the Germania Orchestra, it became the seedbed of similar organizations all over the country. This tradition was carried to the Midwest by Frederick Stock and to Boston by Carl Zerrahn. Others spread this form of cultural expression to additional urban centers throughout the land.

Community singing and glee clubs owe much to the German immigrant, who remembered his singing societies. The first *Männerchor* was founded in Philadelphia in 1835; the first *Liederkranz* was organized in Baltimore in 1836. Their counterparts have been a feature of the German-American community everywhere.

The ideas of German immigrants helped to shape our educational system. They introduced the kindergarten, or "children's play school." They also promoted the concept of the state-endowed university, patterned after the German university. The University of Michigan, founded in 1837, was the first such school to add to the philosophy of general liberal arts education an emphasis upon vocational training. The colonial concept of a university as a place to prepare gentlemen for a life of leisured culture was modified to include training in specialized skills.

---

36 **widespread** (adj.): found over a large area 36 *dissension* (n.): disagreement or quarrelling 37 **oppression** (n.): condition of being unjustly or cruelly ruled 38 *freethinker* (n.): person not accepting traditional religious teaching, but basing his ideas on reason 38 *burgeon* (v.) /ˋbɜdʒən/: begin to grow 41 *mellow* (v.): make or become soft 41 *austere* (adj.): severely moral and strict 41 *imprint* (n.): lasting effect 42 *observe* (v.): celebrate 42 *solemnity* (n.): sacredness 44 *relaxation* (n.): recreation; Entspannung, Erholungspause 47 *celebration* (n.): act of celebrating 49 **trace** (v.): follow or discover (s. b. or s. th.) by observing marks, etc.; follow the development or history of 55 *glee club* (n.): group singing songs 57 **counterpart** (n.): person or thing closely corresponding to another 60 *promote* (v.): further; help to found or organize 61 *state-endowed university*: university which is given money by the state (as against a private university) 63 **emphasis** (n.): (the placing of) special value or importance 63 *vocational* (adj.): of a person's occupation or profession 64 *colonial* (adj.): of a colony or colonies 64 **concept** (n.): general notion.

"The Thing Won't Melt!"

The program of physical education in the schools had its roots in the *Turnverein,* or German gymnastic society. It was adopted and introduced to the American public by the YMCA.

German immigrant influence has been pervasive, in our language, in our mores, in our customs and in our basic philosophy. Even the hamburger, the frankfurter and the delicatessen, that omnipresent neighborhood institution, came to us via the German immigrants.

---

68 *YMCA*: Young Men's Christian Association, organization seeking to improve the spiritual, mental, social, and physical condition of young men; founded 1844 in London, U.S. movement began 1851. By the 1960's the more than 1, 800 YMCA's in the U. S. had a membership of nearly three million. 69 *pervasive* (adj.): tending to spread through every part of 69 *mores* (pl. n.) /ˈmɔreɪz/: (formal) customs, usages, conventions, regarded as essential to a social group 71 *omnipresent* (adj.): present in all places at the same time.

Although they were mostly Democrats prior to 1850, the Germans broke party lines in the decade before the Civil War and played a prominent part in the formation of the Republican party. They were most united on two issues. They opposed the Blue Laws, and they vigorously fought the extension of slavery into new territories. Indeed, the first protest against Negro slavery came from Germantown settlers, led by Franz Pastorius, in 1688.

During the Civil War they fought on both sides. Following the Civil War, Germans infused the faltering American labor movement with new strength by organizing craft unions for printers, watchmakers, carpenters, ironworkers, locksmiths, butchers and bakers.

Adjusting with relative ease, they did not feel the sting of ethnic discrimination until the outbreak of the First World War, when they became targets of wartime hysteria. This hysteria even caused overardent "patriots" to call sauerkraut "Liberty cabbage" and hamburger "Salisbury steak." Nonetheless, when the United States entered the war in 1917, men of German ancestry entered the armed forces of the United States and served with distinction.

As the Second World War drew near, Americans of German descent faced another test. Only a few joined the pro-Nazi German-American Bund, and many of those left as soon as they discovered its real nature. More "older Americans" than those of German descent could be counted in the ranks of America-Firsters. Again, after the U. S. was attacked, descendants of German immigrants fought with valor in our armed services.

---

74 **decade** (n.) /ˈdekeɪd/: period of ten years 76 *Blue Law* (n.): a puritanical law, esp. prohibiting certain activities on Sunday 76 *vigorously* (adv.): strongly, energetically 76 *extension* (n.): extending or being extended 80 *infuse* (v.): inspire; instill or impart qualities, etc. 80 *falter* (v.): move unsteadily; stumble 81 *locksmith* (n.): maker or mender of locks 84 **target** (n.) /ˈtɑgɪt/: object of attack, criticism, etc. 85 *hysteria* (n.) /hɪˈstɪərɪə/: senseless, uncontrolled excitement 85 *overardent* (adj.): excessively full of enthusiasm 87 **ancestry** (n.): line of those persons from whom one is descended; Vorfahren 92 *America-Firsters*: collective name for the members of some parties (the Republican Party, the Union Party, the National Union for Social Justice) who before the Second World War attacked President Roosevelt's New Deal as regimentation and socialism, as did the pro-Nazi German-American Bund. They also opposed America's entry into the war and supported (together with the members of the Bund and a number of Trotskyists) their cause for non-intervention. 93 *valor* (n.) /ˈvælə(r)/: (BE -our) bravery, esp. in war.

14: Chinese Exclusion Act

After the U. S. acquired California (1846 this state exchanged Mexican for American rule, 1848 the peace treaty with Mexico was ratified by the U. S. Senate), the large inflow of Chinese into that state was welcomed at first because of the need for cheap labor. A treaty with China signed in 1868 guaranteed the right of Chinese immigration, but did not guarantee the right of naturalization. In the following decades much anti-Chinese feeling arose in California and a complete ban on Chinese immigration was urged. In a treaty of 1880 China allowed the U. S. some right to restrict, but not to prohibit, Chinese immigration. The Chinese Exclusion Act of 1882 did, however, ban immigration of Chinese laborers for ten years. When that period was up, Congress continued exclusion unilaterally until the Immigration Act of 1924 (cf. text 17) made control automatic. In 1943 the acts were repealed; an annual immigration quota of 105 was set, and citizenship privileges were extended to Chinese.

The following text of the Chinese Exclusion Act (1882) is taken from Henry Steele Commager, ed., *Documents of American History* (New York: Appleton-Century-Crofts, Fifth Edition, 1949), Document 307.

An act to execute certain treaty stipulations relating to Chinese.

WHEREAS, in the opinion of the Government of the United States the coming of Chinese laborers to this country endangers the good order of certain localities within the territory thereof: Therefore,

---

(Title) **exclusion** (n.): refusal to admit; rejection *act* (n.): law.

(Introduction) 2 *ratify* (v.): confirm (an agreement, a treaty, a law) by signature or other formality 3 *inflow* (n.): flowing in 4 **guarantee** (v.) /ˈgærənˋti/: assure that s. th. will be done as specified 5 **immigration** (n.): coming as a settler into another country 5 **naturalization** (n.) /AE ˈnætʃrlɪˋzeɪʃn; BE ˈnætʃrlaɪˋzeɪʃn/: giving (s. b. from another country) rights of citizenship 6 **decade** (n.) /ˋdəkeɪd/: period of ten years 7 *ban* (n.): official prohibition 8 **restrict** (v.): limit; keep within limits 8 **prohibit** (v.) /prəˋhɪbɪt/: forbid (esp. by rules or regulations) 11 *unilateral* (adj.) /ˈjunɪˋlætrl/: affecting one side only; einseitig 12 *automatic* (adj.): self-acting 12 **repeal** (v.): annul (a law, etc.); annullieren, aufheben 12 **quota** (n.): limited number of immigrants allowed to enter a country 13 **privilege** (n.) /ˋprɪvəlɪdʒ/: special favour or benefit.

1 *stipulation* (n.): essential condition of an agreement 2 *whereas* (conj.): (esp. legal) considering that 3 **endanger** (v.): put in danger; gefährden.

Be it enacted, That from and after the expiration of ninety days next after the passage of this act, and until the expiration of ten years next after the passage of this act, the coming of Chinese laborers to the United States be, . . . suspended; and during such suspension it shall not be lawful for any Chinese laborer to come, or, having so come after the expiration of said ninety days, to remain within the United States.

SEC. 2. That the master of any vessel who shall knowingly bring within the United States on such vessel, and land or permit to be landed, any Chinese laborer, from any foreign port or place, shall be deemed guilty of a misdemeanor, and on conviction thereof shall be punished by a fine of not more than five hundred dollars for each and every such Chinese laborer so brought, and may be also imprisoned for a term not exceeding one year.

SEC. 3. That the two foregoing sections shall not apply to Chinese laborers who were in the United States on the seventeenth day of November, eighteen hundred and eighty, or who shall have come into the same before the expiration of ninety days next after the passage of this act, . . .

SEC. 6. That in order to the faithful execution of articles one and two of the treaty in this act before mentioned, every Chinese person other than a laborer who may be entitled by said treaty and this act to come within the United States, and who shall be about to come to the United States, shall be identified as so entitled by the Chinese Government in each case, such identity to be evidenced by a certificate issued under the authority of said government, which certificate shall be in the English language or (if not in the English language) accompanied by a translation into English, stating such right to come, and which certificate shall state the name, title, or official rank, if any, the age, height, and all physical peculiarities, former and present occupation or profession, and place of residence in China of the person to whom the certificate is issued and that such person is entitled conformably to the treaty in this act mentioned to come within the United States. . . .

SEC. 12. That no Chinese person shall be permitted to enter the United States by land without producing to the proper officer of customs the certificate in this act required of Chinese persons seeking to land from a vessel. And any Chinese person found unlawfully within the United States shall be caused to be removed therefrom to the country from whence he came, by direction of the President of the United States, and at the cost of the United States, after being brought before some justice, judge, or commissioner of a court of the United States and found to be one not lawfully entitled to be or remain in the United States.

---

5 *enact* (v.): make (a law) 6 *expiration* (n.) /ˈekspɪˋreɪʃn/: ending (of a period of time) 6 **passage** (n.): passing of a bill so that it becomes a law 7 *suspend* (v.) /səˋspend/: stop for a time 13 *deem* (v.): consider 13 *misdemeanor* (n.) (BE -our) /ˈmɪsdɪˋminə(r)/: (legal) offense less serious than a major crime 13 *conviction* (n.): (of a jury or a judge) declaring in a law court that s. b. is guilty of a crime 15 *term* (n.): fixed or limited period of time 17 *foregoing* (adj.): already mentioned 21 *faithful* (adj.): true to the facts; accurate 24 **identify** (v.) /ɑɪˋdentɪfɑɪ or ɪˋdentɪfɑɪ/: say, show, prove who or what s. b. is 25 **identity** (n.) /ɑɪˋdentətɪ or ɪˋdentətɪ/: who s. b. is 25 **evidence** (v.): prove by evidence (=Beweis, Beweisstück) 28 **certificate** (n.) /səˋtɪfɪkət/: written or printed statement, made by s. b. in authority, that may be used as proof or evidence of s. th. 29 *peculiarity* (n.): Besonderheit 31 *conformable* (adj.): in accordance with 39 *commissioner* (n.): official.

An Anti-Chinese Riot in Denver, Colorado

SEC. 13. That this act shall not apply to diplomatic and other officers of the Chinese Government traveling upon the business of that government, whose credentials shall be taken as equivalent to the certificate in this act mentioned, and shall exempt them and their body and household servants from the provisions of this act as to other Chinese persons.

SEC. 14. That hereafter no State court or court of the United States shall admit Chinese to citizenship; and all laws in conflict with this act are hereby repealed.

SEC. 15. That the words "Chinese laborers," whenever used in this act, shall be construed to mean both skilled and unskilled laborers and Chinese employed in mining.

---

43 *credentials* (pl. n.): letters or papers showing that a person is what he claims to be 43 *equivalent* (adj.) /ɪˈkwɪvələnt/: equal in meaning 44 **exempt from** (v.): free from (an obligation) 44 *provision* (n.): condition in a legal document 49 *construe* (v.): explain the meaning of words, sentences, acts, etc. 50 *mining* (n.): process of digging minerals (gold, silver, etc.) from the earth.

15: WOODROW WILSON: Address to Naturalized Citizens*

Woodrow Wilson, President of the United States (1913–21), addressed four thousand "naturalized citizens" (immigrants upon whom have been conferred the rights of citizenship) in Philadelphia in May 1915.

The following text is taken from Max J. Herzberg, ed., *This Is America* (New York: Pocket Books, 1950), pp. 78–81.

It warms my heart that you should give me such a reception; but it is not of myself that I wish to think tonight, but of those who have just become citizens of the United States.

This is the only country in the world which experiences this constant and repeated rebirth. Other countries depend upon the multiplication of their own native people. This country is constantly drinking strength out of new sources by the voluntary association with it of great bodies of strong men and forward-looking women out of other lands. And so by the gift of the free will of independent people it is being constantly renewed from generation to generation by the same process by which it was originally created. It is as if humanity had determined to see to it that this great nation, founded for the benefit of humanity, should not lack for the allegiance of the people of the world.

You have just taken an oath of allegiance to the United States. Of allegiance to whom? Of allegiance to no one, unless it be to God – certainly not of allegiance to those who temporarily represent this great government. You have taken an oath of allegiance to a great ideal, to a great body of principles, to a great hope of the human race. You have said, "We are going to America not only to earn a living, not only to seek the things which it was more difficult to obtain where we were born, but to help forward the great enterprises of the human spirit – to let men know that everywhere in the world there are men who will cross strange oceans and go where a speech is spoken which is alien to them if they can but satisfy their quest for what their spirits crave; knowing that whatever the speech, there is but one longing and utterance

---

(Title) *address* (n.): speech **naturalize** (v.) /ˈnætʃrlɑɪz/: confer citizenship upon an alien (= foreigner).

(Introduction) 2 **confer s. th. on s. b.** (v.): give or grant.

5 *rebirth* (n.): revival, spiritual change 5 *multiplication* (n.): increasing in number by procreation (= begetting offspring) 6 **voluntary** (adj.) /ˈvolənterɪ/: doing or ready to do things willingly, without being compelled 7 *association* (n.): group of persons joined together for some common purpose 8 *gift* (n.): natural ability 11 **allegiance** (n.) /əˈlidʒəns/: loyalty (to a government) 13 **oath** (n.): solemn declaration that s. th. is true; Eid 19 **enterprise** (n.): undertaking, esp. one that needs courage or that offers difficulty 21 **alien** (adj.) /ˈeɪlɪən/: foreign 21 *quest* (n.): search or pursuit 22 *crave* (v.): have a strong desire for 22 *utterance* (n.): expression; Äußerung.

of the human heart, and that is for liberty and justice." And while you bring all countries with you, you come with a purpose of leaving all other countries behind you – bringing what is best of their spirit, but not looking over your shoulders and seeking to perpetuate what you intended to leave behind in them. I certainly would not be one even to suggest that a man cease to love the home of his birth and the nation of his origin – these things are very sacred and ought not to be put out of our hearts – but it is one thing to love the place where you were born and it is another thing to dedicate yourself to the place to which you go. You cannot dedicate yourself to America unless you become in every respect and with every purpose of your will thorough Americans. You cannot become thorough Americans if you think of yourselves in groups. America does not consist of groups. A man who thinks of himself as belonging to a particular national group in America has not yet become an American, and the man who goes among you to trade upon your nationality is no worthy son to live under the Stars and Stripes.

My urgent advice to you would be, not only always to think first of America, but always, also, to think first of humanity. You do not love humanity if you seek to divide humanity into jealous camps. Humanity can be welded together only by love, by sympathy, by justice, not by jealousy and hatred. I am sorry for the man who seeks to make personal capital out of the passions of his fellowmen. He has lost the touch and ideal of America. For America was created to unite mankind by those passions which lift and not by the passions which separate and debase. We came to America, either ourselves or in the persons of our ancestors, to better the ideals of men, to make them see finer things than they had seen before, to get rid of the things that divide and to make sure of the things that unite. It was but an historical accident no doubt that this great country was called the "United States"; yet I am very thankful that it has that word "United" in its title, and the man who seeks to divide man from man, group from group, interest from interest in this great Union is striking at its very heart.

It is a very interesting circumstance to me, in thinking of those of you who have just sworn allegiance to this great Government, that you were drawn across the ocean by some beckoning finger of hope, by some belief, by some vision of a new kind of justice, by some expectation of a better kind of life. No doubt you have been disappointed in some of us. Some of us are very disappointing. No doubt you have found that justice in the United States goes only with a pure heart and a right purpose as it does everywhere else in the world. No doubt what you found here did not seem touched for you, after all, with the complete beauty of the ideal which you had conceived beforehand. But remember this: If we had grown at all poor in the ideal,

---

26 *perpetuate* (v.) /pəˈpetʃʊeɪt/: continue without interruption 27 **cease** (v.): stop; aufhören 30 **dedicate** (v.): devote 32 *thorough* (adj.) /ˈθʌrə/: complete 35 *trade upon* (v.): take a wrong advantage of 36 Stars and Stripes: the flag of the U. S. 37 *urgent* (adj.): needing prompt decision or action 40 *jealousy* (n.) /ˈdʒeləsɪ/: the feeling or showing of fear or ill will of possible or actual loss of rights or love 39 **weld** (v.): form (pieces of metal) by hammering or pressure when the metal is softened by heat; schweißen 43 **passion** (n.): strong feeling or enthusiasm, esp. of love, hate or anger; Leidenschaft 43 *debase* (v.): make lower in value, dignity, etc. 44 **ancestor** (n.): any one of those persons from whom one is descended, esp. one more remote than a grandparent; Vorfahr 44 *better* (v.): improve 53 *beckon* (v.): summon by a gesture; lure, entice 59 *beforehand* (adv.): earlier, before.

Immigrants salute "Old Glory."

you brought some of it with you. A man does not hope for the thing that he does not believe in, and if some of us have forgotten what America believed in, you, at any rate, imported in your own hearts a renewal of the belief. That is the reason that I, for one, make you welcome. If I have in any degree forgotten what America was intended for, I will thank God if you will remind me. I was born in America. You dreamed dreams of what America was to be, and I hope you brought the dreams with you. No man that does not see visions will ever realize any high hope or undertake any high enterprise. Just because you brought dreams with you, America is more likely to realize dreams such as you brought. You are enriching us if you came expecting us to be better than we are.

You have come into this great nation voluntarily seeking something that we have to give, and all that we have to give is this: We cannot exempt you from work. No man is exempt from work anywhere in the world. We cannot exempt you from the strife and the heartbreaking burden of the struggle of the day – that is common to mankind everywhere; we cannot exempt you from the loads that you must carry. We can only make them light by the spirit in which they are carried. That is the spirit of hope, it is the spirit of liberty, it is the spirit of justice.

---

71 **exempt s. b. from s. th.** (v.): free from (an obligation) 73 *strife* (n.): struggle.

16: ELIAS LIEBERMAN: I Am an American

Elias Lieberman, born in Russia in 1883, was a New York poet, translator, and teacher. His most famous poem "I Am an American" first appeared in *Paved Streets* (1918).

The poem is taken from Carl Van Doren, *The Patriotic Anthology* (Garden City, N. Y.: Doubleday, Doran and Co., 1941), pp. 439–40.

I Am an American

My father belongs to the Sons of the Revolution;
My mother, to the Colonial Dames.
One of my ancestors pitched tea overboard in Boston Harbor;
Another stood his ground with Warren;
Another hungered with Washington at Valley Forge.
My forefathers were America in the making.
They spoke in her council halls;
They died on her battle-fields;
They commanded her ships;
They cleared her forests.
Dawns reddened and paled.
Stanch hearts of mine beat fast at each new star
In the nations's flag.

---

2 *Sons of the Revolution*: Sons of the American Revolution, a national patriotic organization, founded in New York in 1889 by union of Sons of Revolutionary Sires and certain members of the Society of the Sons of the Revolution; membership is open to those whose ancestors saw active service in the Revolutionary forces. 3 *Colonial Dames*: a women organization to the Sons of the Revolution. Today the most influential patriotic society of women are the Daughters of the American Revolution, organized in 1890, open to women whose ancestors aided the patriotic cause in the Revolution. 4 **ancestor** (n.): any one of those persons from whom one is descended, esp. one more remote than a grandparent; Vorfahr 4 *pitch* (v.): throw 5 *Warren*: James Warren (1726–1808), Massachusetts political leader and American patriot, served on the Navy Board (1776–1781); as one of three major-generals of the provincial militia, he led a force into Rhode Island 6 *Valley Forge*: locality in southeast Pennsylvania, northwest of Philadelphia; the main camp of Washington's Continental army was established here (December 1777 – June 1778); troops suffered through severe winter 7 *in the making*: in a stage of development 8 *council hall* (n.): place in which an administrative or legislative body assembles 11 *clear* (v.): lichten, roden 12 *pale* (v.): lose colour 13 *stanch* (adj.) /stæntʃ/ (AE for BE staunch /stɔntʃ/): trustworthy; loyal; firm.

5 T.E.A.S. Bischoff: America, the Melting Pot 41005

Keen eyes of mine foresaw her greater glory:
The sweep of her seas,
The plenty of her plains,
The man-hives in her billion-wired cities.
Every drop of blood in me holds a heritage of patriotism.
I am proud of my past.
I am an American.

I Am an American

My father was an atom of dust,
My mother a straw in the wind,
To His Serene Majesty.
One of my ancestors died in the mines of Siberia;
Another was crippled for life by twenty blows of the knout;
Another was killed defending his home during the massacres.
The history of my ancestors is a trail of blood
To the palace-gate of the Great White Czar.
But then the dream came –
The dream of America.
In the light of the Liberty torch
The atom of dust became a man
And the straw in the wind became a woman
For the first time.

"See," said my father, pointing to the flag that fluttered near,
"That flag of stars and stripes is yours;
It is the emblem of the promised land.
It means, my son, the hope of humanity.
Live for it – die for it!"
Under the open sky of my new country I swore to do so;
And every drop of blood in me will keep that vow.
I am proud of my future.
I am an American.

---

18 *hive* (n.): box for bees to live in; place full of busy people 18 *wire* (v.): install electrical circuits in a building, to provide lighting, power, etc. 19 **heritage** (n.) /ˈherɪtɪdʒ/: that which has been or may be inherited; Erbe 25 *His Serene Majesty*: Seine durchlauchtigste Hoheit; allusion to the emperor of Russia 27 *cripple* (v.): damage seriously; verkrüppeln 27 *knout* (n.) /naʊt): leather whip formerly used in Russia for punishment 28 *massacre* (n.) /ˈmæsəkə(r)/: cruel killing of large numbers of (esp. defenseless) people 33 *Liberty torch*: the torch (=Fackel) the Statue of Liberty holds in her right hand; cf. text 3 37 *flutter* (v.): wehen, flattern 39 *emblem* (n.) /ˈembləm/: symbol 39 **promised land**: the land of promise; the fertile country (Canaan) promised to the Israelites; das gelobte Land; as for the concept of America as the Promised Land, cf. text 2, line 90.

17: Immigration Restriction up to the 1920's

The history of immigration restriction up to the 1920's is summarized by Henry Steele Commager. This summary is followed by an excerpt from the Immigration Act of 1924.

The following texts are taken from Henry Steele Commager, ed., *Documents of American History* (New York: Appleton-Century–Crofts, Fifth Edition, 1949), Documents 422, 453.

Perhaps it is not very generally realized that the per centum limit law marked the beginning of actual restriction or limitation of immigration to the United States from Europe, Africa, Australia, and a considerable part of Asia. The Chinese exclusion act of 1882, the passport agreement with Japan which became effective in 1908, and the "barred zone" provision in the general immigration law of 1917 had already stopped or greatly reduced the influx of oriental peoples, but so far as others, and particularly Europeans, were concerned, all applicants who met the various tests prescribed in the general law, first enacted in 1882 and several times revised and strengthened, was and still is based on the principle of selection rather than of numerical restriction. It is probably true that the provision barring illiterate aliens from admission, which was added to the general law in 1917, was intended as a restrictive measure rather than a quality test, but in its practical effect it was only another addition to the already numerous class of alleged undesirables who were denied admission, and obviously could not be relied upon actually to limit the volume of immigration.

The immigration act of 1882, which, as already indicated, was the first general law upon the subject, provided for the exclusion from the United States of the following classes only: Convicts, lunatics, idiots, and persons likely to become a public charge. This law underwent more or less important revisions in 1891, 1893, 1903, 1907, and 1917, until the last-mentioned act, which is the present general immigration law, denies admission to many classes of aliens, including the following: Idiots, imbeciles, feebleminded persons, epileptics, insane persons; persons who have had one or more attacks of insanity at any time previously; persons of constitutional psychopathic inferiority; persons with chronic alcoholism; paupers; professional beggars; vagrants; persons afflicted with tuberculosis in any form or with a loathsome or dangerous contagious disease; persons certified by the examining physician as being mentally or physically defective, such physical defect being of a nature which may affect the ability of the alien to earn a living; persons who have been convicted of or admit having committed a felony or other crime or misdemeanor involving moral turpitude; polygamists, or persons who practice polygamy or believe in or advocate the practice

---

Consult your dictionary for unknown words.

of polygamy; anarchists and similar classes; immoral persons and persons coming for an immoral purpose; contract laborers; persons likely to become a public charge; persons seeking admission within one year of date of previous debarment or deportation; persons whose ticket or passage is paid for with the money of another or who are assisted by others to come, unless it is affirmatively shown that such persons do not belong to one of the foregoing excluded classes; persons whose ticket or passage is paid for by any corparation, association, society, municipality, or foreign government, either directly or indirectly; stowaways; children under 16 years of age unless accompanied by one or both of their parents; persons who are natives of certain geographically defined territory; aliens over 16 years of age who are unable to read some language or dialect; certain accompanying aliens, as described in the last proviso of section 18 of the act; and persons who have arrived in Canada or Mexico by certain steamship lines. Persons who fail to meet certain passport requirements were added to the excluded classes in subsequent legislation.

Obviously it would be difficult to find, or even to invent, many other terms denoting individual undesirability which might be added to the foregoing list, but, as already pointed out, the general law is essentially selective in theory, for even its most rigid application with respect to the excludable classes above enumerated could not be depended upon to prevent the coming of unlimited numbers of aliens who were able to meet the tests imposed.

Even a casual survey of congressional discussions of the immigration problem during the past quarter of a century demonstrates very clearly that while the law makers were deeply concerned with the mental, moral, and physical quality of immigrants, there developed as time went on an even greater concern as to the fundamental racial character of the constantly increasing numbers who came. The record of alien arrivals year by year has shown a gradual falling off in the immigration of northwest European peoples, representing racial stocks which were common to America even in colonial days, and a rapid and remarkably large increase in the movement from southern and eastern European countries and Asiatic Turkey. Immigration from the last-named sources reached an annual average of about 750.000 and in some years nearly a million came, and there seems to have been a general belief in Congress that it would increase rather than diminish. At the same time no one seems to have anticipated a revival of the formerly large influx from the "old sources," as the countries of northwest Europe came to be known.

This remarkable change in the sources and racial character of our immigrants led to an almost continuous agitation of the immigration problem both in and out of Congress, and there was a steadily growing demand for restriction, particularly of the newer movement from the south and east of Europe. During the greater part of this period of agitation the so-called literacy test for aliens was the favorite weapon of the restrictionists, and its widespread popularity appears to have been based quite largely on a belief, or at least a hope, that it would reduce to some extent the stream of "new" immigration, about one-third of which was illiterate, without seriously interfering with the coming of the older type, among whom illiteracy was at a minimum.

Presidents Cleveland and Taft vetoed immigration bills because they contained a literacy test provision, and President Wilson vetoed two bills largely for the same reason. In 1917, however, Congress passed a general immigration bill which included the literacy provision over the President's veto, and, with certain exceptions, aliens

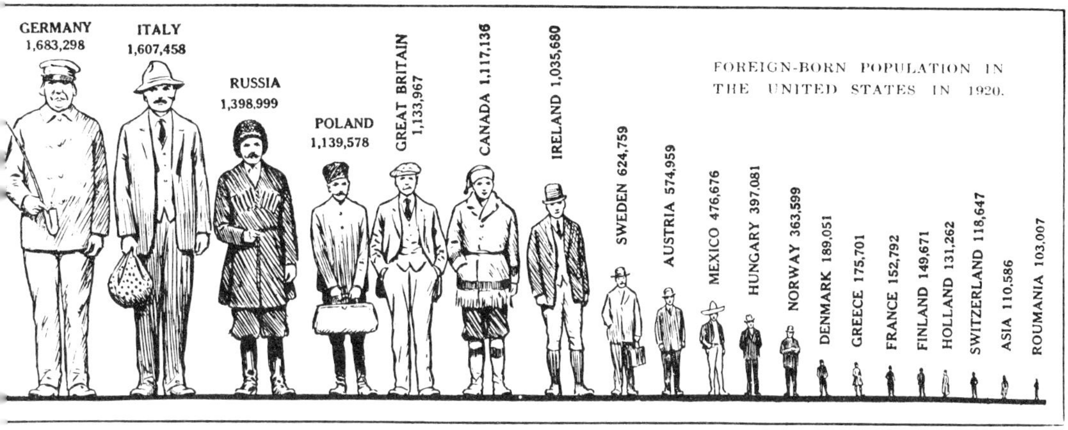

who are unable to read are no longer admitted to the United States. At that time, however, the World War had already had the effect of reducing immigration from Europe to a low level, and our own entry into the conflict a few days before the law in question went into effect practically stopped it altogether. Consequently, the value of the literacy provision as a means of restricting European immigration was never fairly tested under normal conditions.

The Congress, however, seemingly realized that even the comprehensive immigration law of 1917, including the literacy test, would afford only a frail barrier against the promised rush from the war-stricken countries of Europe, and in December, 1920, the House of Representatives, with little opposition, passed a bill to suspend practically all immigration for the time being. The per centum limit plan was substituted by the Senate, however, and the substitute prevailed in Congress, but it failed to become a law at the time because President Wilson withheld executive approval. Nevertheless, favorable action was not long delayed, for at the special session called at the beginning of the present administration the measure was quickly enacted, and, with President Harding's approval, became a law on May 19, 1921. This law expired by limitation June 30, 1922, but by the act of May 11, 1922, its life was extended to June 30, 1924, and some strengthening amendments were added.

The principal provisions of the per centum limit act, or the "quota law," as it is popularly known, are as follows:

The number of aliens of any nationality who may be admitted to the United States in any fiscal year shall not exceed 3 per cent of the number of persons of such nationality who were resident in the United States according to the census of 1910.

Monthly quotas are limited to 20 per cent of the annual quota.

For the purposes of the act, "nationality" is determined by country of birth.

The law does not apply to the following classes of aliens: Government officials; aliens in transit; aliens visiting the United States as tourists or temporarily for business or pleasure; aliens from countries immigration from which is regulated in accordance with treaties or agreement relating solely to immigration, otherwise China and Japan; aliens from the so-called Asiatic barred zone; aliens who have resided continuously for at least five years in Canada, Newfoundland, Cuba, Mexico, Central or South America, or adjacent islands; aliens under the age of 18 who are children of citizens of the United States.

"The only way to handle it!"

Certain other classes of aliens who are counted against quotas are admissible after a quota is exhausted. The following are included in this category: Aliens returning from a temporary visit abroad; aliens who are professional actors, artists, lecturers, singers, ministers of any religious denomination, professors for colleges or seminaries, members of any recognized learned profession, or aliens employed as domestic servants.

So far as possible preference is given to the wives and certain near relatives of citizens of the United States, applicants for citizenship and honorably discharged soldiers, eligible to citizenship, who served in the United States military or naval forces at any time between April 6, 1917, and November 11, 1918.

Transportation companies are liable to a fine of $200 for each alien brought to a United States port in excess of the quota and where such fine is imposed the amount paid for passage must be returned to the rejected alien.

The quota limit law is in addition to and not in substitution for the provisions of the immigration laws.

Immigrant taking an Intelligence Test

Excerpt from the Immigration Act of 1924

BY THE PRESIDENT OF THE UNITED STATES
OF AMERICA
A PROCLAMATION

Whereas it is provided in the act of Congress approved May 26, 1924, entitled "An act to limit the immigration of aliens into the United States, and for other purposes" that –

"The annual quota of any nationality shall be two per centum of the number of foreign-born individuals of such nationality resident in continental United States as determined by the United States census of 1890, but the minimum quota of any nationality shall be 100. . . .

"The Secretary of State, the Secretary of Commerce, and the Secretary of Labor, jointly, shall, as soon as feasible after the enactment of this act, prepare a statement showing the number of individuals of the various nationalities resident in continental United States as determined by the United States census of 1890. . . ."

Now, therefore, I, Calvin Coolidge, President of the United States of America acting under and by virtue of the power in me vested by the aforesaid act of Congress, do hereby proclaim and make known that on and after July 1, 1924, and throughout the fiscal year 1924–1925, the quota of each nationality provided in said Act shall be as follows:

[A selection from the quotas for various countries]

Country or area of birth	Quota for 1924–1925
Afghanistan	100
Albania	100
Andorra	100
Austria	785
Bulgaria	100
Cameroon (proposed British mandate)	100
Cameroon (French mandate)	100
China	100
Czechoslovakia	3,073
Danzig, Free City of	228
Denmark	2,789
Egypt	100
Esthonia	124
Germany	51,227
Great Britain and Northern Ireland	34,007
Greece	100
Hungary	473
Iceland	100
India	100
Iraq (Mesopotamia)	100
Irish Free State	28,567
Italy, including Rhodes, Dodekanesia, and Castellorizzo	3,845
Japan	100
Lithuania	344
Monaco	100
Nepal	100
Netherlands	1,648
Norway	6,453
Poland	5,982
Rumania	603
Russia, European and Asiatic	2,248
Spain	131
Sweden	9,561
Switzerland	2,081
Turkey	100

General note. – The immigration quotas assigned to the various countries and quota-areas should not be regarded as having any political significance whatever, or as involving recognition of new governments, or of new boundaries, or of transfers of territory except as the United States Government has already made such recognition in a formal and official manner. . . .

Calvin Coolidge.

18: ERNEST HEMINGWAY:
I Can Tell Wops a Mile off*

Ernest Hemingway's (1899–1961) *in our time* was published in Paris in 1924, containing only the vignettes or interchapters of the short story collection *In Our Time,* which appeared one year later in the U. S.

The following text is "Interchapter VIII", taken from *In our Time* (New York: Charles Scribner's Sons, 1970), p. 79.

At two o'clock in the morning two Hungarians got into a cigar store at Fifteenth Street and Grand Avenue. Drevitts and Boyle drove up from the Fifteenth Street police station in a Ford. The Hungarians were backing their wagon out of an alley. Boyle shot one off the seat of the wagon and one out of the wagon box. Drevitts got frightened when he found they were both dead. Hell Jimmy, he said, you oughtn't to have done it. There's liable to be a hell of a lot of trouble.

– They're crooks, ain't they? said Boyle. They're wops, ain't they? Who the hell is going to make any trouble?

– That's all right maybe this time, said Drevitts, but how did you know they were wops when you bumped them?

Wops, said Boyle, I can tell wops a mile off.

(Title) *tell* (v.): recognize *wop* (n.) /wʌp/: (derog.) a person of Italian descent.

(Introduction) 2 *vignette* (n.) /viˈnjet/: short literary sketch (= Skizze).

4 *back* (v.): move backward 4 *wagon* (n.): short for station wagon; an automobile with folding or removable rear seats and a back that opens 4 *alley* (n.) /ˈælɪ/: narrow passage between houses or other buildings (often a narrow street in a slum quarter) 7 *be liable to*: be likely to 9 *crook* (n.) /krʊk/: (coll.) person who makes a living by dishonest or criminal means 9 *ain't*: sl. for aren't 12 *bump* (v.): sl. for murder.

19: ELMER RICE: Street Scene

Elmer Rice (1892–1967), a New York dramatist, producer, and novelist, wrote the realistic play *Street Scene* in 1929. It was produced the same year and was awarded the Pulitzer Prize. This play was again successfully produced at a small New York theatre in 1975.

The following section of the play is from Kenneth MacGowan, ed., *Famous Plays of the 1920s* (New York: Dell, 1967), pp. 330–36.

[The play is set in the exterior of a tenement house on Manhattan's Lower East Side. In this brown-stone apartment house live the German Laura Hildebrand and her two children, the Irish family Frank Maurrant (wife Anna, daughter Rose), the Jew Abraham Kaplan with his son Samuel and daughter Shirley, the Italian Filippo Fiorentino and his German wife Greta, the Anglo-Saxon family Jones, and the Scandinavian couple Carl and Olga Olsen. The Hildebrands, who receive money from the "Charities", have been threatened to be evicted, because they do not pay their rent. Miss Simpson from the "Charities" has been in their apartment and is leaving the tenement house.]

Mrs. Maurrant [*as* MISS SIMPSON *comes out of the house*]. Look out, Frank. Let the lady pass.

Miss Simpson. Excuse me.

They make way for her as she comes down the steps. MRS. MAURRANT *seats herself on the stoop.*

Lippo. Meeses Hil'brand, she gotta da tougha luck, ha? Tomorra, dey gonna t'row 'er out in da street, ha?

Miss Simpson [*stopping at the right of the stoop and turning toward him*]. Yes, they are. And if she has any place to sleep, it will only be because the Charities find her a place. And you'd be doing her a much more neighborly act if you helped her

(Introduction) 1 *producer* (n.): Regisseur 3 *award* (v.): give or grant by official decision (e. g. a prize) 3 *Pulitzer Prize* /ˈpjulɪtsə(r)/: prize awarded annually since 1917 by the trustees of Columbia University in New York and the Advisory Board on the Pulitzer Prizes, for achievements in American journalism and letters; they include eight awards in specific fields of journalism, six in letters, and one in musical composition.

(Context) 1 *exterior* (n.): outside 1 **tenement house** (n.) /ˈtenəmənt/: large house for the use of many families at low rents 7 *Charities* (pl. n.): society or organization for helping the poor; Wohlfahrt 7 **evict** (v.): expel a tenant (= Mieter) from a house by authority of the law.

5 *stoop* (n.): small covered entrance at the door of a house.

to realize the value of money, instead of encouraging her to throw it away.

Lippo [*with a deprecatory shrug*]. Ah, lady, no! I give 'er coupla dollar, make 'er feel good, maka me feel good – dat don' 'urt nobody.

SHIRLEY *reappears at the window.*

Miss Simpson. Yes, it does. It's bad for her character.

Kaplan [*throwing away his cigarette and laughing aloud*]. Ha! You mek me leff!

Miss Simpson [*turning angrily*]. Nobody's asking your opinion.

Kaplan. Dot's oll right. I'm taling you vit'out esking. You hoid maybe already dot poem:

Orgenized cherity, measured and iced,
In der name of a kushus, stetistical Christ.

Miss Simpson [*fiercely*]. All the same, you Jews are the first to run to the Charities.

She strides angrily off at the right. LIPPO, *affecting a mincing gait, pretends to follow her.*

Kaplan [*leaning out of the window*]. Come back and I'll tal you somet'ing vill maybe do good your kerecter.

Mrs. Fiorentino. Lippo!

Mrs. Jones [*highly amused*]. Look at him, will ya?

Lippo [*laughing and waving his hand*]. Gooda-by, lady! [*He comes back to the stoop.*]

Kaplan [*to the others*]. Dey toin out in de street a mudder vit' two children, and dis female comes and preaches to her bourgeois morelity.

Mrs. Jones [*to* MRS. FIORENTINO]. He's shootin' off his face again.

Shirley. Papa, it's time to go to bed!

Kaplan [*irritably*]. Lat me alone, Shoiley. [*Rising and addressing the others.*] Dees cherities are notting but anudder dewise for popperizing de verking klesses. Ven de lendlords steal from de verkers a million dollars, dey give to de Cherities a t'ousand.

Maurrant. Yeah? Well, who's puttin' her out on the street? What about the lan'lord here? He's a Jew, ain't he?

Mrs. Jones. I'll say he's a Jew! Isaac Cohen!

Kaplan. Jews oder not Jews – vot has dis got to do vit' de quastion? I'm not toking releegion, I'm toking economics. So long as de kepitalist klesses –

Maurrant [*interrupting*]. I'm talkin' about if you don't pay your rent, you gotta move.

Mrs. Maurrant. It doesn't seen right, though, to put a poor woman out of her home.

Mrs. Fiorentino. And for her husband to run away – dot vos not right either.

Lippo. I betcha 'e's got 'nudder woman. He find a nice blonda chicken, 'e run away.

Mrs. Jones. There ought to be a law against women goin' around stealin' other women's husbands.

---

12 *deprecatory* (adj.) /ˋdeprəkəˈtərɪ/: expressing disapproval 12 *shrug* (n.): lifting the shoulders slightly to show indifference, doubt, etc. 16 *leff*: Kaplan's pronunciation of AE laugh /læf/ 18 *hoid*: heard; in lower class New York City sociolect the ɜ-sound is pronounced as ɔɪ, e. g. shirt /ʃɔɪt/, girl /gɔɪl/, turn /tɔɪn/. 24 *affect* (v.): pretend 24 *mincing* (adj.): delicate 24 *gait* (n.): manner of walking or running 36 *popperize* =pauperize (v.): bring to the state of being a pauper (person without means or livelihood).

Tenement House Yard on the Lower East Side

Mrs. Fiorentino. Yes, dot's right, Mrs. Jones.

Maurrant. Well, what I'm sayin' is, it ain't the landlord's fault.

Kaplan. Eet's de folt of our economic system. So long as de institution of priwate property exeests, de verkers vill be at de moicy of de property-owning klesses.

Maurrant. That's a lot o' bushwa! I'm a woikin' man, see? I been payin' dues for twenty-two years in the Stagehands Union. If we're not gettin' what we want, we call a strike, see? – and then we get it.

Lippo. Sure! Ees same wit' me. We gotta Musician Union. We getta pay for da rehears', we getta pay for da overtime –

Shirley. That's all right when you belong to a strong union. But when a union is weak, like the Teachers' Union, it doesn't do you any good.

Mrs. Jones [*to* Mrs. Fiorentino]. Can y' imagine that? Teachers belongin' to a union!

---

54 *bushwa* (n.) /ˈbʊʃwa/: AE sl. for bunk, baloney, blah; Quatsch 54 *dues* (pl. n): sums of money to be paid for membership; Mitgliedsbeitrag 55 *Stagehands Union:* Gewerkschaft der stagehands; stagehand: one who sets up scenery, furniture, lights, etc. for a stage play 58 rehears': rehearsal (n.) /rɪˈhɜsl/: practising a play for public performance; Probe.

Kaplan [*impatiently*]. Oll dese unions eccomplish notting votever. Oll dis does not toch de fondamental problem. So long as de tuls of industry are in de hands of de kepitalist klesses, ve vill hev exploitation and sloms and –

Maurrant. T' hell wit' all dat hooey! I'm makin' a good livin' an' I'm not doin' any kickin'.

Olsen [*removing his pipe from his mouth*]. Ve got prosperity, dis coontry.

Jones. You said somethin'!

Kaplan. Sure, for de reech is planty prosperity! Mister Morgan rides in his yacht and upstairs dey toin a voman vit' two children in de street.

Maurant. And if you was to elect a Socialist president tomorra, it would be the same thing.

Mrs. Fiorentino. Yes, dot's right, Mrs. Maurrant.

Jones. You're right!

Kaplan. Who's toking about electing presidents? Ve must put de tuls of industry in de hends of de verking klesses, and dis ken be accomplished only by a sushal revolution!

Maurrant. Yeah? Well, we don't want no revolutions in this country, see?

General chorus of assent.

Mrs. Jones. I know all about that stuff – teachin' kids there ain't no Gawd an' that their gran'fathers was monkeys.

Jones [*rising angrily*]. Free love, like they got in Russia, huh?

KAPLAN *makes a gesture of impatient disgust and sinks back into his chair.*

Maurrant. There's too goddam many o' you Bolsheviks runnin' aroun' loose. If you don't like the way things is run here, why in hell don't you go back where you came from?

Shirley. Everybody has a right to his own opinion, Mr. Maurrant.

Maurrant. Not if they're against law and order, they ain't. We don't want no foreigners comin' in, tellin' us how to run things.

Mrs. Fiorentino. It's nothing wrong to be a foreigner. Many good people are foreigners.

Lippo. Sure! Looka Eetalians. Looka Cristoforo Colombo! 'E'sa firs' man discov' America – 'e's Eetalian, jussa like me.

Maurrant. I'm not sayin' anythin' about that –

Olsen [*removing his pipe*]. Firs' man is Lief Ericson.

Lippo [*excitedly, going toward* OLSEN]. Wassa dat?

Olsen. Firs' man is Lief Ericson.

Lippo. No! No! Colombo! Cristoforo Colomb' – 'e'sa firs' man discov' America – ever'body knowa dat! [*He looks around appealingly.*]

Mrs. Jones. Why, sure, everybody knows that.

Jones. Every kid learns that in school.

---

66 *hooey* (n.): AE sl. for nonsense, baloney, bunk 67 *kick* (v.): AE sl. for complain 77 *klesses*: Kaplan's pronunciation of AE classes /ˈklæsəs/ 80 *assent* (n.): agreement 81 *teachin' kids . . . that their gran'fathers was monkeys*: an allusion (= Anspielung) to the Scopes trial of 1925. John T. Scopes of Dayton, Tennessee, a public-school teacher, was tried for teaching Darwinian theory contrary to state statute and convicted.

Shirley. Ericson was really the first discoverer –

Lippo [*yelling*]. No! Colomb'!

Shirley. But Columbus was the first to open America to settlement.

Lippo [*happily, as he goes back to the stoop*]. Sure, dassa wot Ahm say – Colomb' is firs'.

Olsen. Firs' man is Lief Ericson.

Lippo [*tapping his forehead significantly*]. Looka wot Eetalian do for America – 'e build bridge, 'e build railroad, 'e build subway, 'e dig sewer. Wit'out Eetalian, ees no America.

Jones. Like I heard a feller sayin': the Eye-talians built New York, the Irish run it, an' the Jews own it. [*Laughter.*]

Mrs. Fiorentino [*convulsed*]. Oh! Dot's funny!

Jones [*pleased with his success*]. Yep, the Jews own it all right.

Maurrant. Yeah, an' they're the ones that's doin' all the kickin'.

Shirley. It's no disgrace to be a Jew, Mr. Maurrant.

Maurrant. I'm not sayin' it is. All I'm sayin' is, what we need in this country is a little more respect for law an' order. Look at what's happenin' to people's homes, with all this divorce an' one thing an' another. Young girls goin' around smokin' cigarettes an' their skirts up around their necks. An' a lot o' long-haired guys talkin' about free love an' birth control an' breakin' up decent people's homes. I tell you it's time somethin' was done to put the fear o' God into people!

Mrs. Jones. Good for you, Mr. Maurrant!

Jones. You're damn right.

Mrs. Fiorentino. Dot's right, Mr. Maurrant!

Mrs. Maurrant. Sometimes, I think maybe they're only trying to get something out of life.

Maurrant. Get somethin', huh? Somethin' they oughtn't to have, is that it?

Mrs. Maurrant. No; I was only thinking –

Maurrant. Yeah, you were only thinkin', huh?

Kaplan [*rising to his feet again*]. De femily is primerily an economic institution.

Mrs. Jones [*to* MRS. FIORENTINO]. He's in again.

Kaplan. Ven priwate property is ebolished, de femily will no longer hev eny reason to exeest.

Shirley. Can't you keep quiet, Papa?

Maurrant [*belligerently*]. Yeah? Is that so? No reason to exist, huh? Well, it's gonna exist, see? Children respectin' their parents an' doin' what they're told, get me? An' husbands an' wives lovin' an' honorin' each other, like they said they would when they was spliced – an' any dirty sheeny that says different is li'ble to get his head busted open, see?

Mrs. Maurrant [*springing to her feet*]. Frank!

Shirley [*trying to restrain* KAPLAN]. Papa!

Kaplan. Oll right! I should argue vit' a low-kless gengster.

---

112 *feller* (n.): AE dialect for fellow 114 *convulse* (v.) cause to shake with laughter, rage, etc. 115 *yep*: AE sl. for yes 137 *belligerent* (adj.) /bɪˈlɪdʒərənt/: kampflustig 140 *splice* (v.): AE sl. for marry.

Hester Street on the Lower East Side

Maurrant [*raging*]. Who's a gangster? Why, you goddamn –! [*He makes for the balustrade.*

Mrs. Maurrant [*seizing his arm*]. Frank!

Jones [*seizing the other arm*]. Hey! Wait a minute! Wait a minute!

Maurrant. Lemme go!

Shirley [*interposing herself*]. You should be ashamed to talk like that to an old man! [*She slams down the window.*]

Maurrant. Yeah? [*To* MRS. MAURRANT *and* JONES.] All right, lemme go! I ain't gonna do nothin'.

They release him. SHIRLEY *expostulates with* KAPLAN *and leads him away from the window.*

---

150 *interpose* (v.): say s. th. as an interruption.

Mrs. Jones [*who has run over to the right of the stoop*]. Maybe if somebody handed him one, he'd shut up with his talk for a while.

Lippo. 'E talka lika dat een Eetaly, Mussolini's gonna geeve 'eem da castor-oil.

Mrs. Jones [*laughing*]. Yeah? Say, that's a funny idea!

[*Still chuckling, she goes back to the railing at the left of the stoop.*]

Jones. No kiddin', is that what they do?

Mrs. Fiorentino. Yes, dot's true. My husband read it to me in the Italian paper.

Mrs. Maurrant. Why must people always be hurting and injuring each other? Why can't they live together in peace?

Maurrant [*mockingly*]. Live in peace! You're always talkin' about livin' in peace!

Mrs. Maurrant. Well, it's true Frank. Why can't people just as well be kind to each other?

Maurrant. Then let 'im go live with his own kind.

Jones [*coming down the steps*]. Yeah, that's what I say. [*As* Mrs. Jones *laughs aloud.*] What's eatin' you?

Mrs. Jones. I was just thinkin' about the castor-oil. [Maurrant *seats himself on the right balustrade.*]

Lippo. Sure, 'esa funny fell', Mussolini. [*Doubling up in mock pain.*] 'E geeve 'em da pain in da belly, dey no can talk.

---

158 *castor-oil* (n.): thick, yellowish oil, made from beans of the castor (= Rizinus) plant, used as a purgative; Verdauungsmittel 170 *what's eatin'* you?: what's worrying you? 172 *balustrade* (n.) /ˈbæləˋstreɪd/: railing held up by banisters (= posts supporting the hand-rail of a staircace) 173 *double up* (v.): bend the body with pain or in helpless laughter.

20: MICHAEL GOLD: Hunting with Buffalo Bill in Italian Territory*

Michael Gold, pseudonym of Irwin Granich (1893–1967), was born and reared on New York's Lower East Side. His experience of the slums and as a worker led him to become a Communist. In 1930, at the beginning of the depression, his semi-autobiographical work *Jews without Money* was published.

The following text is from Michael Gold, *Jews without Money* (New York: Avon Books, 1965), pp. 132–136.

THE Jewish holidays were fascinating to children. It was like having a dozen Christmases during the year. I liked the Hanukah candle festival, and the joy at the Jewish New Year. I liked the romantic Succoth feast, when primitive shacks roofed with bulrushes were built in the tenement yards, for East Side Jews to feast in as a memory of their wander-years in the Arabian desert.

The synagogue services were amusing at times. It was like a theater. The Rabbi blew a ram's horn, and a hundred bearded men wrapped in shrouds convulsed them-

---

(Title) *Buffalo Bill*: real name William Frederick Cody (1846–1917); served as a frontier scout during the Civil War, and again from 1868 to 1872, as well as in the battles against the Sioux. In 1883 he started his famous "Wild West Show", the prototype of many later ones, and he had previously acted in Western melodramas. The dime novels of Ned Buntline and Prentiss Ingraham are partially responsible for his popular reputation (cf. annotation to line 38 of this text). **territory** (n.) /ˋterətɔrɪ/: land or district.

(Introduction) 1 *pseudonym* (n.) /ˋsjudənɪm/: name taken, esp. by an author, instead of his real name 2 Lower East Side: section of Manhattan where first-generation immigrants used to live from about 1880 to 1914; see map on p. 85 3 **depression** (n.): period of reduced business, much unemployment, etc. 4 *semi-autobiographical* (adj.) /semɪˌɔtəˈbaɪəˋgræfɪkl/: zum Teil autobiographisch.

1 *fascinate* (v.) /ˋfæsɪneɪt/: charm or attract greatly 2 *Hanukah candle festival* /khɑnʊkɑ/: in Hebrew "Hanukah" means "dedication" (= Weihung), a Jewish festival commemorating the rededication of the Temple in Jerusalem by Judas Maccabaeus in 165 B. C. and celebrated for eight days beginning the 25th day of Kislev (the third month of the Jewish year) in late September 3 the Jewish New Year: the Jewish calendar differs from our calendar. The Jewish year has only 354 days consisting of twelve months and begins in late September 3 *Succoth* (n.) /sʊkɔt/: the Feast of Tabernacles (= Laubhüttenfest), celebrating the fall harvest and commemorating the desert wandering of the Jews during the Exodus (= Auszug aus Ägypten) 4 *bulrush* (n.) /ˋbʊlrʌʃ/: (kinds of) tall rush or reed with a thick velvety head; Schilfrohr, Binse 4 **tenement** (n.) /ˋtenəmənt/: large house for the use of many families at low rents 4 *feast* (v.): take part in a religious anniversary or festival 6 *synagogue* (n.) /ˋsɪnəgɔg/: (building used for an) assembly of Jews for religious teaching and worship 6 *Rabbi* (n.) /ˋræbaɪ/: (title of a) spiritual leader of a Jewish congregation 7 *ram's horn*: Widderhorn; Schofar used as a musical instrument in a Jewish religious ceremony 7 *shroud* (n.): (fig.) Gewand 7 *convulse* (v.): shake violently.

selves in agony. They groaned, sobbed, beat their breasts and wailed those strange Oriental melodies, that are two thousand years old, yet still move the Jewish heart.

A boy was awed by this passion. But mostly the congregation droned through hours and hours of meaningless Hebrew. The synagogues stank with bad air; the windows were always locked. People gossiped, yawned, belched, took snuff, talked business, and spat on the floor. Even the grown-ups were bored. And so a boy wriggled from his father's side, and rolled dice for picture buttons with other bored youngsters in the hallway.

My interest in the Messiah began on a summer day. My gang had gone off to fish for lafayettes at some river dock, and I had missed them. I was all alone on my street, and there was nothing to do. I walked down to the Bowery; here there was always something exciting.

I lingered around the doors of saloons. I heard men shouting inside, and pianos going. Then I dared to stroll a little further down, to the ten- and twenty-cent lodging houses. Bums in blue cotton shirts lounged around; one of them glared at me and I ran away. I came to the employment agencies. Here I watched the pullers-in at work. They bullied the big laborers in overalls who wandered past. They snatched them out of their aimless dreaming before the signboards and dragged them inside, to be shipped off on some job.

I spelled out the chalk writing on the signboards: 60 Men Wanted for Lumber Camp Upstate; Men Wanted for Section Gangs. I wondered what section gangs were like, and lumber camps. Then I saw two drunken men in overalls punching at each other. One slipped. The other kicked at his face until it was a bloody mash. A cop

---

8 *agony* (n.) /ˈægənɪ/: great pain or suffering (of mind and body) 8 *wail* (v.): cry or complain in a loud, usu. shrill, voice 10 *awed* (adj.): filled with respect combined with fear and reverence 10 **congregation** (n.): body of people taking part in religious worship 10 *drone* (v.): talk or sing in a low, monotonous way 12 **gossip** (v.): talk idly; talk about the affairs of other people 12 *belch* (v.): rülpsen 12 *snuff* (n.): Schnupftabak 13 *spit, spat, spat* (v.): spucken 13 **bore** (v.): make s. b. feel tired by being dull or tedious; langweilen 13 *wriggle* (v.): move with quick, short twistings 14 *dice* (pl. n.): Würfel 14 *picture button* (n.): small disk with a picture on it that can be worn like a button 15 *hallway* (n.): passageway or room between the entrance and the interior of a building 16 *Messiah* (n.) /məˈsaɪə/: meaning "der Gesalbte" in Hebrew, the promised and expected deliverer of the Jews; for Christians, Jesus Christ is regarded as the realization of the Messianic prophecy. 16 **gang** (n.): group of persons going about together; Bande 17 *lafayette* (n.): any kind of small fish 17 *dock* (n.): Anlegeplatz für Schiffe 18 *Bowery*: (from the Dutch word meaning "farm" or "plantation") a street in Lower Manhattan, characterized by flophouses, saloons, etc.; cf. map on p. 85 20 *linger* (v.): loiter, hang around 20 *saloon* (n.): AE: place where alcoholic drinks are sold and drunk; bar 21 **stroll** (v.): walk about leisurely 21/22 *lodging house* (n.): house in which rooms are let (usu. by the week) 22 *bum* (n.) (coll.) vagrant; loafer 22 *lounge around* (v.): move, sit, lie, etc., in a relaxed way; spend time in idleness 22 *glare* (v.): stare 23 *employment agency* (n.): Büro für Arbeitsvermittlung 23 *puller-in* (n.): person who draws in or holds back 24 *bully* (v.) /ˈbʊlɪ/: use one's strength to frighten or hurt those who are weaker 24 *overalls* (pl. n.): Arbeitsanzug 25 *signboard* (n.): advertisement (painted on a board) 26 *ship* (v.): send or transport by any carrier 27/28 Lumber Camp Upstate: camp in upstate New York where timber is cut down and sawed into lumber (= beams, planks, boards, etc.) 28 *Section Gang* (n.): a crew of men (section hands) who do the maintenance work on a railroad section 29 *punch* (v.): strike hard with the fist 30 *mash* (n.): any soft mass 30 *cop* (n.) /kʌp/: AE coll. for policeman.

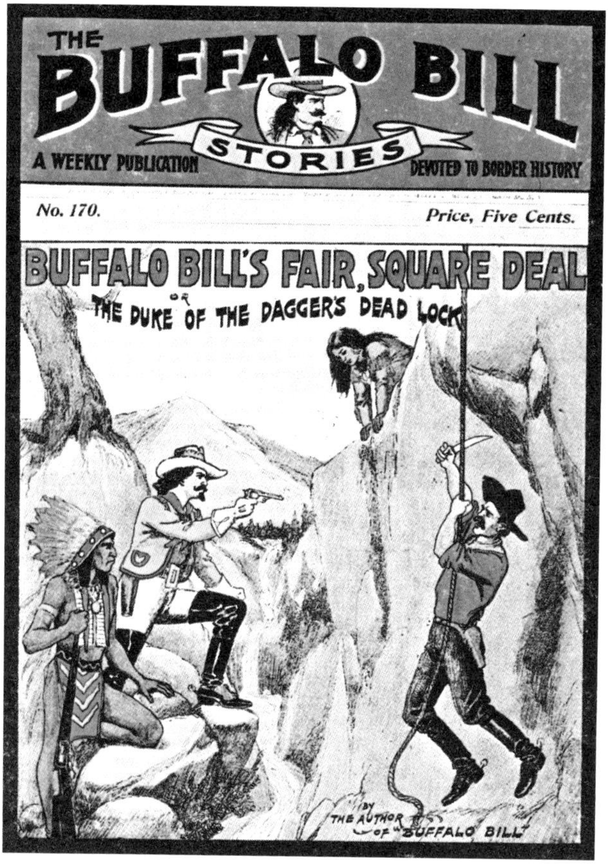

arrested them. A police wagon clanged its way to the curbing, and they were flung in like dogs. A crowd hooted and laughed as they were driven off.

I had two pennies. I decided to go to Chinatown and buy some sugar-cane. This would be a great adventure. I would see if I were brave. I would go there by way of Mulberry Street. That was the land of the hereditary enemy – the Italians lived there. I might be killed. But Buffalo Bill would have gone by way of Mulberry Street. I must make myself as brave as Buffalo Bill. He was my hero then; I was reading the

---

31 *wagon* (n.) /ˈwægən/: short for station wagon, an automobile with folding or removable rear seats and a back that opens 31 *clang* (v.): make a loud ringing sound 31 *curbing* (n.): concrete edging along a street; Bordsteinkante 32 *hoot* (v.): shout or cry expressing disapproval or scorn 33 *penny* (n.): a U. S. cent 33 *Chinatown:* Chinese quarter on Manhattan's Lower East Side; cf. map on p. 85 33 *sugar-cane* (n.): Zuckerrohr 35 Mulberry Street: Street in Manhattan's Little Italy; cf. map on p. 85 35 **hereditary** (adj.) /hɪˈredəterɪ/: passed on from parent to child, from one generation to following generations; hereditary enemy = Erbfeind.

gaudy little paper books that described his adventures.

I walked down Hester Street toward Mulberry. Yes, it was like the Wild West. Under the fierce sky Buffalo Bill and I chased buffalo over the vast plains. We shot them down in hundreds. Then a secret message was sent us from a beautiful white maiden. She was a prisoner in the camp of the Indians. The cruel redskins were about to torture her. Buffalo Bill and I rode and rode and rode. In the nick of time we saved her. Two hundred cruel redskins bit the dust before our trusty rifles. We escaped with the white girl, and rode and rode and rode.

So why should I fear these Italian boys? I saw two of them rolling an iron hoop down the street. My knees shook. I pretended to myself I was a spy and walked along as if I belonged here. I looked around carelessly. I saw the Italian pushcarts. They were heaped with strange green vegetables I had never seen. I saw an old Italian man who wore earrings. I saw Christians eating oysters and clams at a pushcart; I had heard of this, but not believed it. I saw a pig's head on exhibition in a butcher's window; another dirty but fascinating object eaten by Christians.

Bang. I had been slugged over the head. I jumped in surprise and turned to see who had hit me. I was in the hands of the enemy! Eight Italian boys with sticks surrounded me, whooping like Indians. Their eyes gleamed, their faces were cruel. The thing I feared most had happened.

The leader, a big strong boy, clutched my collar, and asked fiercely:

"What streeter?"

I was confused, and made a great tactical blunder. I told the truth.

"Chrystie Street," I said.

"Hooray, a Jew, a Jew!" he screamed, his face lighting up with a boy's joyous cruelty. He slugged me with his stick. The others yelled and joined in the slugging. I fell to the pavement, then fought to my feet and ran. Down Mulberry Street I ran. They pursued me, throwing stones, bricks and vegetables.

---

38 *the gaudy little paper books*: dime novels (= Groschenromane), published weekly, were very popular with American youngsters in the late 19th and early 20th centuries. Ned Buntline (real name Edward Zane Carroll Judson) was one of the creators of this genre, the other was Prentiss Ingraham. In 1869 Buntline met William F. Cody (cf. annotation to this text's title), and, endowing him with the name Buffalo Bill, made him the hero of a series of dime novels. Ingraham wrote about 200 dime novels about his friend Buffalo Bill; cf. illustration on p. 83 39 *Hester Street*: street in the Jewish quarter on the Lower East Side, famous for its street market; cf. illustrations on p. 79 and the cover of this book 40 *buffalo* (pl. n.): North American bison; Büffel 40 **plains** (pl. n.): sloping region of valleys and plains in West Central North America, extending from Texas north to South Alberta; the Great Plains 42 *maiden* (n.): (poet.) girl; young unmarried woman 42 *redskin* (n.): Indian 43 *in the nick of time*: only just in time; at the critical or opportune time 44 *bite the dust* (v.): AE Western sl. for die 44 *trusty rifle*: dependable rifle; sichere Büchse; 46 *hoop* (n.): Rad; Reifen 48 *pushcart* (n.): cart used by hand, esp. one used by street vendors (= Verkäufer, Händler) 49 *heap* (v.): pile up 50 *Christians eating oysters and clams*: the Jewish dietary laws (= religiöse Ernährungsvorschriften) forbid the eating of oysters (= Austern) and clams (= Muscheln) 51 *exhibition* (n.): Auslage 53 *bang*: (echoic) a loud and hard hit or blow 53 *slug* (v.): (coll.) hit hard with the fist 55 *whoop* (v.): cry out 55 *gleam* (v.): shine with a flash of light 57 *clutch* (v.): grasp or hold tightly 58 *what streeter?*: what street do you live on? 59 *tactical* (adj.): taktisch 59 *blunder* (n.): foolish mistake 60 *Chrystie Street*: street in the Jewish quarter on the Lower East Side; cf. map on p. 85 61 *hooray* (interj.): shout of joy or approval 62 *yell* (v.): cry out loudly; scream 62 *join in s. th.* (v.): take part in.

The Lower East Side around 1910

"Christ-killer!" some one yelled. All the boys took up the ancient cry. The mob grew; there must have been fifty boys chasing me now. A stone caught me on the temple, and I tasted blood on my lips. A brick cut my right shin. My ribs were bruised by the sticks; my shirt slimy with horse-dung and rotten vegetables. I couldn't breathe; my lungs pricked me like needles.

The grown-ups lined the curbing and watched the chase without much interest. Some of them laughed at the juvenile tragedy. I sobbed and ran. I grew weaker. At last I came to the Bowery, and managed to cross it into my own Jewish land.

The Italians were afraid to follow me across the Bowery; some of my own gang might attack them here. They remained on their own side, and yelled a last exultant "Christ-killer!" as they watched me trot safely home.

I sat in my mother's lap, sobbing, while she washed away the blood and filth. She scolded me, kissed me, and cursed the bad Christians who had done this.

"Who is Christ, momma?"

"It is their false Messiah!" said my mother, bitterly.

"But I didn't kill him! Why do they say I killed him?"

"Of course you didn't kill him, darling. Don't cry so. The Christians killed him, and now they blame us for it."

"But who was Christ, momma?"

"He was a bad magician who wanted to make the Jews believe he was the Messiah. But we laughed at him, so he hated us, and betrayed his own race to the Gentiles."

"And he really wasn't the Messiah?"

"Of course not. When the Messiah comes he will save the world. He will make everything good. That false Messiah made things only worse. Look at the world; liars and thieves everywhere, wars, murders and children killed with street cars! When the true Messiah comes he will change all this."

"When will he come, momma?"

"I don't know. Ask Reb Samuel; maybe he can tell you."

The thing pressed on my mind. I asked Reb Samuel in his umbrella store that afternoon. He said the Messiah might not come for many years. He would ride a white horse and put to shame every enemy of the Jews.

Would he look like Buffalo Bill? I asked.

No. He would be pale, young and peaceful. He would not shoot people down, but would conquer them with love.

I was disappointed. I needed a Messiah who would look like Buffalo Bill, and who could annihilate our enemies. I had many talks with Reb Samuel about this.

---

65 *mob* (n.): disorderly, lawless crowd 67 *temple* (n.): flat surface beside the forehead in front of each ear 67 *shin* (n.): front part of the leg between the knee and the ankle 68 *bruise* (v.) /bruz/: hurt; injure 68 *slimy* (adj.): moist, slippery 68 *horse-dung* (n.): Pferdekot 70 *line* (v.): form a line along 71 **juvenile** (adj.) /AE`dʒuvənl; BE`dʒuvənaɪl/: of or for young persons 74 *exultant* (adj.) /ɪg`zʌltənt/: rejoicing; triumphant 75 *trot* (v.): run with short steps 76 **filth** (n.): disgusting dirt 77 **scold** (v.): blame with angry words; ausschimpfen 78 *momma* (n.) /`mʌmə/: AE familiar term for mother 84 *magician* (n.) /mə`dʒɪʃn/: person skilled in the art of controlling events by the pretended use of supernatural forces 85 *Gentile* (n.) /`dʒentaɪl/: person not of the Jewish race 89 *killed with*: incorrect for killed by 89 *street car (n.):* AE for BE tram; large coach or car on rails that provides public transportation; Straßenbahn 92 *Reb* (n.): (Yiddish) a Jewish title of respect equivalent to Mister, used with the given name 95 *put to shame* (v.): beschämen 100 *annihilate* (v.) /ə`naɪəleɪt/: destroy completely; vernichten.

21: HENRY ROTH: Arriving in the Golden Land*

Henry Roth was born in 1906 and came to America when he was eighteen months old. His only novel *Call It Sleep* (1934) is generally recognized as a masterpiece of psychological fiction. The novel, after a "Prologue", tells the story of David Schearl's life in the slums of New York's Lower East Side between the ages of six and nine. David, except in the "Prologue", is the novel's center of consciousness.

The following "Prologue", taken from *Call It Sleep* (New York: Avon Books, 1964), pp. 9–16, establishes the emotional pattern that is to dominate the child's life. It describes the meeting on Ellis Island in 1907 between Albert Schearl, a Polish Jewish immigrant already working in New York as a printer, and his wife and infant son who have followed him to join him in America.

(I pray thee ask no questions
this is that Golden Land)

The small white steamer, Peter Stuyvesant, that delivered the immigrants from the stench and throb of the steerage to the stench and the throb of New York tenements, rolled slightly on the water beside the stone quay in the lee of the weathered barracks and new brick buildings of Ellis Island. Her skipper was waiting for the last of the officials, laborers and guards to embark upon her before he cast off and started for Manhattan. Since this was Saturday afternoon and this the last trip she would make for the week-end, those left behind might have to stay over till Monday. Her whistle bellowed its hoarse warning. A few figures in overalls sauntered from the high doors of the immigration quarters and down the grey pavement that led to the dock.

It was May of the year 1907, the year that was destined to bring the greatest number of immigrants to the shores of the United States. All that day, as on all the days since spring began, her decks had been thronged by hundreds upon hundreds of foreigners, natives from almost every land in the world, the jowled close-cropped Teuton, the

(Introduction) 8 **dominate** (v.): have control 9 *Ellis Island*: the U.S.A.'s chief immigration station from 1892 to 1943, situated southwest of Manhattan.

2 *stench* (n.): horrid smell 2 *throb* (n.): beating more rapidly than usual; pulsation 2 **steerage** (n.): that part of a ship nearest the rudder; this section formerly used for providing for passengers travelling at the lowest fares 2 **tenement** (n.) /ˋtenəmənt/: large house for the use of many families at low rents 3 *quay* (n.) /ki/: landing-place, alongside which ships can be tied up for loading and unloading; Kai 3 *lee* (n.): the side or part away from the wind 3 *barrack* (n.): any building of plain and ugly appearance 4 *skipper* (n.): captain, esp. of a small ship 5 **embark** (v.): go on board a ship 8 *bellow* (v.): make a loud, deep noise; roar; shout 8 *hoarse* (adj.): (of the voice) rough and harsh 8 *overalls* (pl. n.): Arbeitsanzug 8 *saunter* (v.): walk in a leisurely way 12 *throng* (v.): crowd 13 *jowled* (adj.): of the lower jaw with the chin and cheeks 13 *close-cropped*: short-cut 13 *Teuton* (n.) /ˋtjutn/: member of a group of north European peoples, esp. a German.

full-bearded Russian, the scraggly-whiskered Jew, and among them Slovack peasants with docile faces, smooth-cheeked and swarthy Armenians, pimply Greeks, Danes with wrinkled eyelids. All day her decks had been colorful, a matrix of the vivid costumes of other lands, the speckled green-and-yellow aprons, the flowered kerchief, embroidered homespun, the silver-braided sheepskin vest, the gaudy scarf, yellow boots, fur caps, caftans, dull gabardines. All day the guttural, the high-pitched voices, the astonished cries, the gasps of wonder, reiterations of gladness had risen from her decks in a motley billow of sound. But now her decks were empty, quiet, spreading out under the sunlight almost as if the warm boards were relaxing from the strain and the pressure of the myriads of feet. All those steerage passengers of the ships that had docked that day who were permitted to enter had already entered – except two, a woman and a young child she carried in her arms. They had just come aboard escorted by a man.

About the appearance of these late comers there was very little that was unusual. The man had evidently spent some time in America and was now bringing his wife and child over from the other side. It might have been thought that he had spent most of his time in lower New York, for he paid only the scantest attention to the Statue of Liberty or to the city rising from the water or to the bridges spanning the East River – or perhaps he was merely too agitated to waste much time on these wonders. His clothes were the ordinary clothes the ordinary New Yorker wore in that period – sober and dull. A black derby accentuated the sharpness and sedentary pallor of his face; a jacket, loose on his tall spare frame, buttoned up in a V close to the throat; and above the V a tightly-knotted black tie was mounted in the groove of a high starched collar. As for his wife, one guessed that she was a European more by the timid wondering look in her eyes as she gazed from her husband to the harbor, than by her clothes. For her clothes were American – a black skirt, a white shirt-waist and a black jacket.

---

14 *scraggly* (adj.): uneven, thin (in growth) 15 *docile* (adj.) /BE`dəʊsaɪl; AE `dosl/: easily trained or controlled 15 *swarthy* (adj.) /`swɔðɪ/: having a dark complexion 15 *pimply* (adj.): having small, hard, inflamed spots on the skin; pickelig 16 *wrinkled* (adj.): having small folds or lines in the skin (esp. of the kind produced by age) 16 *eyelid* (n.): upper or lower covering of the eye 16 *matrix* (n.): that in which s. th. originates, takes form, etc. 16 **vivid** (adj.): bright, intense 17 *speckled* (adj.): marked with small coloured spots 17 *kerchief* (n.) /`kɜtʃɪf/: square piece of cloth or lace used by women as a head covering 18 *embroider* (v.): ornament cloth with needlework 18 *homespun* (n.): cloth made of yarn spun at home 18 *braid* (v.): interweave three or more strands of cloth, etc. 18 *gaudy* (adj.): too bright and showy 18 *scarf* (n.): long strip of material (silk, wool, etc.) worn over the shoulders, round the neck or (by women) over the hair 19 *caftan* (n.) /`kæftən/: long tunic with a girdle at the waist, worn by men in the Near East 19 *gabardines* (pl. n.) /ˈgæbə`dinz/: garments made of wool, cotton, rayon, etc. twilled on one side and having a fine, diagonal weave 19 *guttural* (adj.) /`gʌtərəl/: produced in the throat; rasping 19 *high-pitched* (adj.): (of sounds) shrill 20 *reiteration* (n.): repetition 21 *motley* (adj.): of varied character or various sorts 21 *billow* (n.): anything that sweeps along like a great wave 23 *myriad* (n.) /`mɪrɪəd/: a great number of persons or things 25 *escort* (v.): accompany 30 *scant* (adj.): not quite up to full measure; knapp 31 *span* (v.): extend across (from side to side) 32 *agitated* (adj.): excited 34 *derby* (n.) /`dɜbɪ/: stiff felt hat with a round crown; BE bowler (hat) 34 *accentuate* (v.) /ək`sentʃʊeɪt/: unterstreichen, betonen 34 *sedentary* (adj.) /`sednˈterɪ/: marked by much sitting 34 *pallor* (n.): paleness (esp. of the face) 36 *mount* (v.): put and fix in position 36 *groove* (n.): Furche, Rille 36 *starch* (v.): make a shirt collar stiff with starch (= Stärke).

Obviously her husband had either taken the precaution of sending them to her while she was still in Europe or had brought them with him to Ellis Island where she had slipped them on before she left.

Only the small child in her arms wore a distinctly foreign costume, an impression one got chiefly from the odd, outlandish, blue straw hat on his head with its polka dot ribbons of the same color dangling over each shoulder.

Except for this hat, had the three newcomers been in a crowd, no one probably, could have singled out the woman and child as newly arrived immigrants. They carried no sheets tied up in huge bundles, no bulky wicker baskets, no prized feather beds, no boxes of delicacies, sausages, virgin-olive oils, rare cheeses; the large black satchel beside them was their only luggage. But despite this, despite their even less than commonplace appearance, the two overalled men, sprawled out and smoking cigarettes in the stern, eyed them curiously. And the old peddler woman, sitting with basket of oranges on knee, continually squinted her weak eyes in their direction.

The truth was there was something quite untypical about their behavior. The old peddler woman on the bench and the overalled men in the stern had seen enough husbands meeting their wives and children after a long absence to know how such people ought to behave. The most volatile races, such as the Italians, often danced for joy, whirled each other around, pirouetted in an ecstasy; Swedes sometimes just looked at each other, breathing through open mouths like a panting dog; Jews wept, jabbered, almost put each other's eyes out with the recklessness of their darting gestures; Poles roared and gripped each other at arm's length as though they meant to tear a handful of flesh; and after one pecking kiss, the English might be seen gravitating toward, but never achieving an embrace. But these two stood silent, apart; the man staring with aloof, offended eyes grimly down at the water – or if he turned his face toward his wife at all, it was only to glare in harsh contempt at the blue straw hat worn by the child in her arms, and then his hostile eyes would sweep about the deck to see if anyone else were observing them. And his wife beside him regarding him uneasily, appealingly. And the child against her breast looking from one to the other with watchful, frightened eyes. Altogether it was a very curious meeting.

They had been standing in this strange and silent manner for several minutes, when the woman, as if driven by the strain into action, tried to smile, and touching her

---

40 *precaution* (n.): care taken in advance to avoid a risk 44 *outlandish* (adj.): strange or foreign 44/45 *polka dot* (attrib.): regular pattern of large dots on cloth 48 *bulky* (adj.): taking up much space 48 *wicker* (attrib.): twings or canes woven together, usu. for baskets and furniture 49 *satchel* (n.): small bag for carrying light articles 51 *sprawl out* (v.): sit or lie with the arms and legs loosely spread out 52 *stern* (n.): rear end of a ship or boat 52 *peddler* (n.): person who goes from house to house to sell small articles 53 *squint* (v.): peer with the eyes partly closed 57 *volatile* (adj.) /AE `volətl; BE `volətɑɪl/: (of a person) lively, changing quickly or easily from one mood or interest to another 58 *whirl* (v.): move quickly round and round 58 *pirouette* (v.): dance a pirouette, whirling on one foot or the point of a toe 58 *ecstasy* (n.): (feeling of) great joy and spiritual uplift 59 *pant* (v.) /pænt/: take short, quick breaths; gasp 60 *jabber* (v.): talk excitedly; talk in what seems to be a rapid and confused manner 60 *recklessness* (n.): not thinking of the consequences 60 *dart* (v.): move forward suddenly and quickly 61 **gesture** (n.) /`dʒestʃə(r)/: movement of the hand or head to indicate or illustrate an idea, feeling, etc. 61 *roar* (v.): laugh boisterously; make a loud, deep, rumbling sound 62 *peck* (v.): (coll.) give a quick, casual kiss 63 *gravitate* (v.): move or be attracted 63 *embrace* (n.): Umarmung 65 *harsh* (adj.): stern; cruel; severe 66 *sweep about* (v.): umherstreifen.

husband's arm said timidly, "And this is the Golden Land." She spoke in Yiddish.

The man grunted, but made no answer.

She took a breath as if taking courage, and tremulously, "I'm sorry, Albert, I was so stupid." She paused waiting for some flicker of unbending, some word, which never came. "But you look so lean, Albert, so haggard. And your mustache – you've shaved."

His brusque glance stabbed and withdrew. "Even so."

"You must have suffered in this land." She continued gentle despite his rebuke. "You never wrote me. You're thin. Ach! Then here in the new land is the same old poverty. You've gone without food. I can see it. You've changed."

"Well that don't matter," he snapped, ignoring her sympathy. "It's no excuse for your not recognizing me. Who else would call for you? Do you know anyone else in this land?"

"No," placatingly. "But I was so frightened, Albert. Listen to me. I was so bewildered, and that long waiting there in that vast room since morning. Oh, that horrible waiting! I saw them all go, one after the other. The shoemaker and his wife. The coppersmith and his children from Strij. All those on the Kaiserin Viktoria. But I – I remained. To-morrow will be Sunday. They told me no one could come to fetch me. What if they sent me back? I was frantic!"

"Are you blaming me?" His voice was dangerous.

"No! No! Of course not Albert! I was just explaining."

"Well then let me explain," he said curtly. "I did what I could. I took the day off from the shop. I called that cursed Hamburg-American Line four times. And each time they told me you weren't on board."

"They didn't have any more third-class passage, so I had to take the steerage –"

"Yes, now I know. That's all very well. That couldn't be helped. I came here anyway. The last boat. And what do you do? You refused to recognize me. You don't know me." He dropped his elbows down on the rail, averted his angry face. "That's the greeting I get."

"I'm sorry, Albert," she stroked his arm humbly. "I'm sorry."

"And as if those blue-coated mongrels in there weren't mocking me enough, you give them that brat's right age. Didn't I write you to say seventeen months because it would save the half fare! Didn't you hear me inside when I told them?"

"How could I, Albert?" she protested. "How could I? You were on the other side of that – that cage."

---

72 *Yiddish*: language of the majority of Jews in Eastern Europe until the Second World War; it is a hybrid (= mixed) Germanic language with Hebrew and Slavonic components, written in Hebrew characters 73 *grunt* (v.): make a low, rough sound (as animals, esp. pigs) expressing disagreement, boredom, etc. 74 *tremulous* (adj.): trembling 75 *flicker* (n.): flashing and dying away by turns 75 *unbending* (n.): releasing from tension 76 *lean* (adj.): with little flesh or fat; thin 76 *haggard* (adj.): having a wasted, worn look; hager, abgehärmt 76 *mustache* (n.) /ˈmʌstæʃ/: Schnurrbart 78 *brusque* (adj.) /brusk/: (of speech and behaviour) rough and abrupt 79 *rebuke* (n.): Vorwurf 82 *snap* (v.): speak or utter sharply 85 *placate* (v.): soothe; pacify; beschwichtigen 90 *frantic* (adj.): wildly excited with joy, pain, anxiety, etc. 93 *curt* (adj.): shortspoken; hardly polite 99 *avert* (v.): turn away 102 *mongrel* (n.): a dog of mixed breed 103 *brat* (n.): (contemptuous) child.

"Well why didn't you say seventeen months anyway? Look!" he pointed to several blue-coated officials who came hurrying out of a doorway out of the immigration quarters. "There they are." An ominous pride dragged at his voice. "If he's among them, that one who questioned me so much. I could speak to him if he came up here."

"Don't bother with him, Albert," she exclaimed uneasily. "Please, Albert! What have you against him? He couldn't help it. It's his work."

"Is it?" His eyes followed with unswerving deliberation the blue-coats as they neared the boat. "Well he didn't have to do it so well."

"And after all, I did lie to him, Albert," she said hurriedly trying to distract him.

"The truth is you didn't," he snapped, turning his anger against her. "You made your first lie plain by telling the truth afterward. And made a laughing-stock of me!"

"I didn't know what to do." She picked despairingly at the wire grill beneath the rail. "In Hamburg the doctor laughed at me when I said seventeen months. He's so big. He was big when he was born." She smiled, the worried look on her face vanishing momentarily as she stroked her son's cheek. "Won't you speak to your father, David, beloved?"

The child merely ducked his head behind his mother.

His father stared at him, shifted his gaze and glared down at the officials, and then, as though perplexity had crossed his mind he frowned absently. "How old did he say he was?"

"The doctor? Over two years – and as I say he laughed."

"Well what did he enter?"

"Seventeen months – I told you."

"Then why didn't you tell them seventeen –" He broke off, shrugged violently. "Baah! You need more strength in this land." He paused, eyed her intently and then frowned suddenly. "Did you bring his birth certificate?"

"Why – " She seemed confused. "It may be in the trunk – there on the ship. I don't know. Perhaps I left it behind." Her hand wandered uncertainly to her lips. "I don't know. Is it important? I never thought of it. But surely father could send it. We need only write."

"Hmm! Well, put him down." His head jerked brusquely toward the child. "You don't need to carry him all the way. He's big enough to stand on his own feet."

She hesitated, and then reluctantly set the child down on the deck. Scared, unsteady, the little one edged over to the side opposite his father, and hidden by his mother, clung to her skirt.

"Well, it's all over now." She attempted to be cheerful. "It's all behind us now, isn't it, Albert? Whatever mistakes I made don't really matter any more. Do they?"

"A fine taste of what lies before me!" He turned his back on her and leaned morosely against the rail. "A fine taste!"

---

109 *ominous* (adj.): of bad omen; threatening 113 *unswerving* (adj.): not changing; straight 113 *deliberation* (n.): carefulness; slowness 117 laughing-stock (n.): object of ridicule 118 wire grill (n.): Drahtzaun 121 *momentarily* (adv.): in an instant; for a short time 122 *beloved* (n.) /bɪˈlʌvɪd/: (person) dearly loved, darling 123 *duck* (v.): move quickly down (to avoid being seen or hit) 124 *gaze* (n.): long, steady look 124 *glare* (v.): stare angrily or fiercely 125 *perplexity* (n.): cause of bewilderment 137 *jerk* (v.): twist 139 **reluctant** (adj.): unwilling 140 *edge over* (v.): move gradually.

An Italian immigrant family stands on the deck of a ferry boat plying between Ellis Island, first stop for European immigrants, and New York City.

They were silent. On the dock below, the brown hawsers had been slipped over the mooring posts, and the men on the lower deck now dragged them dripping from the water. Bells clanged. The ship throbbed. Startled by the hoarse bellow of her whistle, the gulls wheeling before her prow rose with slight creaking cry from the green water, and as she churned away from the stone quay skimmed across her path on indolent, scimitar wing. Behind the ship the white wake that stretched to Ellis Island grew longer, raveling wanly into melon-green. On one side curved the low drab Jersey coast-line, the spars and masts on the waterfront fringing the sky; on the other side was Brooklyn, flat, water-towered; the horns of the harbor. And before them, rising on her high pedestal from the scaling swarmy brilliance of sunlit water to the west, Liberty. The spinning disk of the late afternoon sun slanted behind her, and to those on board who gazed, her features were charred with shadow, her depths exhausted, her masses ironed to one single plane. Against the luminous sky the rays of her halo were spikes of darkness roweling the air; shadow flattened the torch she bore to a black cross against flawless light – the blackened hilt of a broken sword. Liberty. The child and his mother stared again at the massive figure in wonder.

The ship curved around in a long arc toward Manhattan, her bow sweeping past Brooklyn and the bridges whose cables and pillars superimposed by distance, spanned the East River in diaphanous and rigid waves. The western wind that raked the harbor into brilliant clods blew fresh and clear–a salt tang in the lull of its veerings. It whipped the polka-dot ribbons on the child's hat straight out behind him. They caught his father's eye.

"Where did you find that crown?"

Startled by his sudden question his wife looked down. "That? That was Maria's parting gift. The old nurse. She bought it herself and then sewed the ribbons on. You don't think it's pretty?"

---

146 *hawser* (n.): thin steel cable (used on ships) 147 *mooring* (n.): making a boat secure to land by means of cables 148 *clang* (v.): make a loud ringing sound 148 *throb* (v.): beat, esp. more rapidly than usual 149 *wheel* (v.): turn in a curve or circle 149 *prow* (n.) /praʊ/: pointed front of a ship or boat 149 *creak* (v.): make a sound like that of an unoiled door-hinge 151 *churn* (v.): stir or move about violently 150 *skim* (v.): move lightly over (a surface) 151 *indolent* (adj.): lazy; inactive 151 *scimitar* (n.) /ˋsɪmɪtə(r)/: short, curved, single-edged sword as formerly used by Persians, Arabs and Turks 151 *wake* (n.): track left by a ship on smooth water 152 *ravel* (v.): separate into its parts; untwist; fray 152 *wan* (adj.) /wɔn/: (of light) pale; not bright 152 *drab* (adj.): dull, yellowish-brown 153 *spar* (n.): strong wooden or metal pole used as a mast, yard, boom, etc. 153 *waterfront* (n.): land at the water's edge, esp. the part of a town facing the sea, the harbour, etc. 153 *fringe* (v.): mit Fransen versehen; umgrenzen 155 *pedestal* (n.) /ˋpedɪstl/: base for a statue 155 *scale* (v.): climb up 155 *swarmy* (adj.): crowded (as with a swarm of bees) 155 *brilliance* (n.): radiance, splendour 156 *Liberty*: Statue of Liberty; for explanation cf. text 3 156 *disk* (n.): thin, flat, round plate 156 *slant* (v.): slope 157 *char* (v.): make or become black by burning 158 *luminous* (adj.) /ˋlumɪnəs/: giving out light; bright 159 *halo* (n.) /ˋheɪləʊ/: Heiligenschein 159 *spike* (n.): pointed piece of metal 159 *rowel* (v.) /ˋraʊəl/: spur or prick (a horse, etc.) with or as with a rowel (= Sporenrad) 160 *hilt* (n.): handle of a sword 162 *arc* (n.): curved line; Bogen 162 *bow* (n.) /baʊ/: front or forward end of a boat or ship 162 *sweep* (v.): pass quickly; move steadily with speed 163 *cable* (n.): thick, strong rope of wire 163 *pillar* (n.): upright column of stone, metal, etc. 163 *superimpose* (v.) /ˈsupərɪmˋpəʊz/: put (one thing) on top of s. th. else 164 *diaphanous* (adj.) /daɪˋæfənəs/: transparent; translucent 164 *rigid* (adj.): stiff 164 *rake* (v.): rechen 165 *clod* (n.): lump (of earth, clay, etc.) 165 *veer* (v.): change direction.

"Pretty? Do you still ask?" His lean jaws hardly moved as he spoke. "Can't you see that those idiots lying back there are watching us already? They're mocking us! What will the others do on the train? He looks like a clown in it. He's the cause of all this trouble anyway!"

The harsh voice, the wrathful glare, the hand flung toward the child frightened him. Without knowing the cause, he knew that the stranger's anger was directed at himself. He burst into tears and pressed closer to his mother.

"Quiet!" the voice above him snapped.

Cowering, the child wept all the louder.

"Hush, darling!" His mother's protecting hands settled on his shoulders.

"Just when we're about to land!" her husband said furiously "He begins this! This howling! And now we'll have it all the way home, I suppose! Quiet! You hear?"

"It's you who are frightening him, Albert!" she protested.

"Am I? Well, let him be quiet. And take that straw gear off his head."

"But Albert, it's cool here."

"Will you take that off when I –" A snarl choked whatever else he would have uttered. While his wife looked on aghast, his long fingers scooped the hat from the child's head. The next instant it was sailing over the ship's side to the green waters below. The overalled men in the stern grinned at each other. The old orange-peddler shook her head and clucked.

"Albert!" his wife caught her breath. "How could you?"

"I could!" he rapped out. "You should have left it behind!" His teeth clicked, and he glared about the deck.

She lifted the sobbing child to her breast, pressed him against her. With a vacant stunned expression, her gaze wandered from the grim smouldering face of her husband to the stern of the ship. In the silvery-green wake that curved trumpet-wise through the water, the blue hat still bobbed and rolled, ribbon stretched out on the waves. Tears sprang to her eyes. She brushed them away quickly, shook her head as if shaking off the memory, and looked toward the bow. Before her the grimy cupolas and towering square walls of the city loomed up. Above the jagged roof tops, the white smoke, whitened and suffused by the slanting sun, faded into the slots and wedges of the sky. She pressed her brow against her child's, hushed him with whispers. This was that vast incredible land, the land of freedom, of immense opportunity, that

---

176 *harsh* (adj.): rough and disagreeable 176 *wrathful* (adj.) /AE ˋræθfəl; BE ˋroθfəl/: zornig 180 *cower* (v.) /ˋkaʊə(r)/: shrink back from fear 181 *hush* (interj.): be silent! 185 *gear* (n.) /gɪə(r)/: clothing 188 *aghast* (adv.): filled with fear 188 *scoop* (v.): take up or out as with a scoop (= Schaufel) 191 *cluck* (v.): make the noise made by a hen 193 *rap out* (v.): say (s. th.) suddenly and sharply 193 *click* (v.): make a short, sharp sound 195 *vacant* (adj.) /ˋveɪkənt/: showing no sign of thought and interest; leer 196 *stunned* (adj.): shocked 196 *smoulder* (v.): burn and smoke without flame; schwelen 198 *bob* (v.): move with a jerky motion 200 *grimy* (adj.): covered with dirt 200 *cupola* (n.) /ˋkjupələ/: small dome forming (part of) a roof; Kuppel 201 *loom* (v.): come into sight indistinctly, esp. in a large and threatening form 201 *jagged* (adj.) /ˋdʒægɪd/: with rough uneven edges 202 *suffuse* (v.): spread slowly over the surface of 202 *slot* (n.): narrow opening through which s. th. is to be put; Schlitz 203 *wedge* (n.): Keil 204 **incredible** (adj.): difficult to believe; unglaublich.

Golden Land. Again she tried to smile.

"Albert," she said timidly, "Albert."

"Hm?"

"Gehen vir voinen du? In Nev York?"

"Nein. Bronzeville. Ich hud dir schoin geschriben."

She nodded uncertainly, sighed . . .

Screws threshing, backing water, the Peter Stuyvesant neared her dock – drifting slowly and with canceled momentum as if reluctant.

---

211 *screw* (n.): Schiffsschraube 211 *thresh* (v.): toss about violently; dreschen 212 **cancel** (v.) /ˈkænsl/: do away with 212 *momentum* (n.): impetus of a moving object.

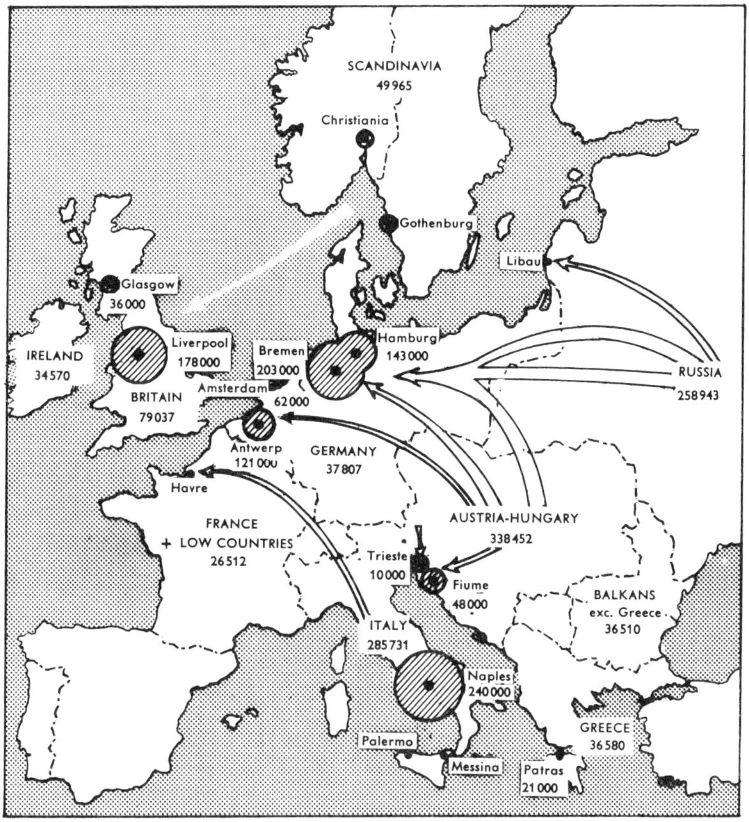

European Emigration to the U.S.A., 1907

22: JOHN F. KENNEDY:
Kennedy's Stand on Immigration*

John F. Kennedy, President of the United States (1961–63), did quite a lot to liberalize the United States' immigration policy.

The following is a chapter from his *A Nation of Immigrants* (New York: Harper and Row, 1964), pp. 77–83.

The Immigration and Nationality Act of 1952 undertook to codify all our national laws on immigration. This was a proper and long overdue task. But it was not just a housekeeping chore. In the course of the deliberation over the Act, many basic decisions about our immigration policy were made. The total racial bar against the naturalization of Japanese, Koreans and other East Asians was removed, and a minimum annual quota of one hundred was provided for each of these countries. Provision was also made to make it easier to reunite husbands and wives. Most important of all was the decision to do nothing about the national origins system.

The famous words of Emma Lazarus on the pedestal of the Statue of Liberty read: "Give me your tired, your poor, your huddled masses yearning to breathe free." Until 1921 this was an accurate picture of our society. Under present law it would be appropriate to add: "as long as they come from Northern Europe, are not too tired or too poor or slightly ill, never stole a loaf of bread, never joined any questionable organization, and can document their activities for the past two years."

Furthermore, the national origins quota system has strong overtones of an indefensible racial preference. It is strongly weighted toward so-called Anglo-Saxons,

---

(Title) *stand* (n.): view, opinion **immigration** (n.): coming as a settler into another country.

(Introduction) 2 **liberalize** (v.): make less strict.

1 **act** (n.): law 1 *codify* (v.): arrange laws systematically 2 *overdue* (adj.): beyond the time fixed; überfällig 3 *chore* (n.): ordinary everyday task 3 *deliberation* (n.): careful consideration and discussion 3 *basic* (adj.): fundamental 4 *racial* (adj.): relating to race 4 *bar* (n.): barrier or obstacle 5 **naturalization** (n.) /AE ˈnætʃrlɪˈzeɪʃn; BE – lɑɪˈz –/: giving or being given rights of citizenship 6 **quota** (n.): limited share, amount or number of immigrants allowed to enter a country 7 provision (n.): condition in a legal document 7 *reunite* (v.): bring or come together again 9 *Emma Lazarus*: cf. text 3 9 *pedestal* (n.) /ˈpedɪstl/: base for a statue 9 *Statue of Liberty*: cf. text 3 10 *huddle* (v.): crowd together 10 **yearn** (v.): be filled with longing or desire 11 *accurate* (adj.): free from error 12 **appropriate** (adj.): fitting; angebracht 13 *loaf* (n.): a portion of bread baked in one piece 14 **document** (v.) /ˈdokjʊmənt/: prove or support by documents 15 *overtones* (pl. n.): implications 16 *indefensible* (adj.): that cannot be defended, justified, or excused 16 *preference* (n.) /ˈprefərəns/: the favouring of one person, race, etc. more than another 16 *weight* (v.): give an extra advantage.

a phrase which one writer calls "a term of art" encompassing almost anyone from Northern and Western Europe. Sinclair Lewis described his hero, Martin Arrowsmith, this way: "a typical pure-bred-Anglo-Saxon American – which means that he was a union of German, French, Scotch-Irish, perhaps a little Spanish, conceivably of the strains lumped together as 'Jewish,' and a great deal of English, which is itself a combination of primitive Britain, Celt, Phoenician, Roman, German, Dane and Swede."

Yet, however much our present policy may be deplored, it still remains our policy. As President Truman said when he vetoed the Immigration and Nationality Act (only to have that veto overridden): "The idea behind this discriminatory policy was, to put it boldly, that Americans with English or Irish names were better people and better citizens than Americans with Italian or Greek or Polish names. . . . Such a concept is utterly unworthy of our traditions and our ideals."

Partly as a result of the inflexibility of the national origins quota system, the government has had to resort to temporary expedients to meet emergency situations. The 1957 Kennedy amendment, which permitted alien spouses, parents and children with inconsequential disqualifications to enter the United States, was responsive to this need. In 1948 Congress passed the Displaced Persons Act allowing more than 400,000 people made homeless by the war to come to this country. In 1953 Congress passed the Refugee Relief Act to admit about 200,000 people, most of whom had fled from behind the Iron Curtain. Under this Act and under a clause of the Immigration and Nationality Act of 1952, not originally intended for use in such situations, some thirty thousand Freedom Fighters from Hungary were admitted in 1957. As a result it became necessary to pass a special law in 1958 to regularize the status of many of these immigrants.

Following the 1958 earthquakes in the Azores which left so many Portuguese homeless, none of these people could enter the United States as quota immigrants. Persons of Dutch origin in the Netherlands who were displaced from Indonesia were also ineligible to enter the United States as quota immigrants. Both needs were met by the Pastore-Kennedy-Walter Act of 1958 admitting a number of them on a

---

17 *encompass* (v.) /ɪnˋkʌmpəs/: comprise 18 *Sinclair Lewis*: (1885–1951), American novelist, who in 1930 became the first American author to be awarded the Nobel Prize; his novel *Arrowsmith* (1925) is on the career of a man of science. 20 *conceivable* (adj.): that can be understood or believed 21 *strain* (n.): line of descent; Abstammung 21 *lump together* (v.): put together in a lump (= Haufen); include (a number of things) under one heading 24 *deplore* (v.): regret; bedauern 25 *veto* (v.) /ˋvitəʊ/: ein Veto einlegen 26 *override* (v.): prevail over 26 **discriminato**ry (adj.) /dɪsˋkrɪmɪnəˈtɔrɪ/: showing discrimination or bias; diskriminierend 27 *bold* (adj.): impudent; clear 28 **concept** (n.): general notion 30 *inflexibility* (n.): rigidity 31 *resort to* (v.): make use of for help (or to gain one's purpose); zurückgreifen auf 31 *expedient* (n.): plan, action, device 31 *meet* (v.): satisfy (a demand, etc.) 31 **emergency** (n.): serious happening needing prompt action 32 **amendment** (n.): revision or change proposed or made in a bill, law, etc. 32 **alien** (adj.) /ˋeɪlɪən/: foreign 32 *spouse* (n.) /spɑʊs/: (one's) husband or wife 33 *inconsequential* (adj.): unimportant 33 *disqualification* (n.): making or declaring unfit 33 *responsive* (adj.): answering 34 *displaced person* (n.): refugee left homeless, unable or unwilling to return to his own country 36 **refugee** (n.) /ˋrefjʊdʒi/: Flüchtling 40 *regularize* (v.): make lawful or correct 45 *ineligible* (adj.): not suitable or qualified.

nonquota basis into the United States. In 1962 a special law had to be passed to permit the immigration of several thousand Chinese refugees who had escaped from Communist China to Hong Kong. The same legislative procedure was used as in the 1957 Hungarian program. Each world crisis is met by a new exception to the Immigration and Nationality Act of 1952. Each exception reflects the natural humanitarian impulses of the American people, which is in keeping with our traditions of shelter to the homeless and refuge for the oppressed.

While none of these measures are, of themselves, especially generous responses to the tremendous problems to which they are addressed, they all have a great impact on our foreign policy. They demonstrate that there is still a place in America for people fleeing from tyranny or natural calamity. Nevertheless, the effect of these actions is diluted by the very fact that they are viewed as exceptions to our national policy rather than as a part of that policy.

Another measure of the inadequacy of the Immigration and Nationality Act has been the huge volume of private immigration bills introduced in Congress. These are bills to deal with individual hardship cases for which the general law fails to provide. In the Eighty-seventh Congress over 3,500 such bills were introduced. Private immigration bills make up about half of our legislation today.

It is not hard to see why. A poor European college girl was convicted three times for putting slugs in a pay telephone, and fifteen years later, married to an American teacher abroad, she was denied entrance to our country because of three separate convictions for a crime involving moral turpitude. Or another case: An Italian immigrant living in Massachusetts with his small children could not bring his wife to the United States because she had been convicted on two counts involving moral turpitude. Her crimes? In 1913 and 1939 she had stolen bundles of sticks to build a fire. It took acts of Congress to reunite both these families.

These are examples of the inadequacies of the present law. They are important of themselves because people's lives are affected by them. But they are more important for what they represent of the way America looks at the world and the way America looks at itself.

There is, of course, a legitimate argument for some limitation upon immigration. We no longer need settlers for virgin lands, and our economy is expanding more slowly than in the nineteenth and early twentieth centuries. A superficial analysis of the heated arguments over immigration policy which have taken place since 1952

---

49 **legislative** (adj.) /ˋledʒɪsˈleɪtɪv/: (of) law making; gesetzgebend 49 *procedure* (n.) /prəˋsi-dʒə(r)/: (the regular) order of doing things, esp. legal and political 51 *humanitarian* (adj.): helping humanity 53 **oppress** (v.): keep down by unjust and cruel use of authority 54 *measures* (pl. n.): course of action 55 *impact* (n.): strong impression or effect 56 **demonstrate** (v.): show clearly by giving proof or example 57 **tyranny** (n.) /ˋtɪrənɪ/: cruel and unjust government 57 *calamity* (n.): great and serious misfortune or disaster 58 *dilute* (v.) /dɑɪˋljut/: weaken the force of 60 *inadequacy* (n.): insufficiency; not being enough for what is required 61 *volume* (n.): large mass, amount, or quantity 61 **introduce** (v.): (ein Gesetz) einbringen 62 *hardship* (n.): severe suffering 65 *convict* (v.): declare in a law court that s. b. is guilty (of a crime) 66 *slug* (n.): piece of metal shaped like and used in place of a coin, esp. such a substitute coin when used illegally 68 *turpitude* (n.): moral corruptness 78 **virgin** (adj.): untouched, unused, pure; jungfräulich 79 **superficial** (adj.): not thorough or profound; oberflächlich.

might give the impression that there was an irreconcilable conflict, as if one side wanted to go back to the policy of our founding fathers, of unrestricted immigration, and the other side wanted to stop all further immigration. In fact, there are only a few basic differences between the most liberal bill offered in recent years, sponsored by former Senator Herbert H. Lehman, and the supporters of the status quo. The present law admits 156,700 quota immigrants annually. The Lehman bill (like a bill introduced by Senator Philip A. Hart and cosponsored by over one-third of the members of the Senate) would admit 250,000.

The clash of opinion arises not over the number of immigrants to be admitted, but over the test for admission – the national origins quota system. Instead of using the discriminatory test of where the immigrant was born, the reform proposals would base admission on the immigrant's possession of skills our country needs and on the humanitarian ground of reuniting families. Such legislation does not seek to make over the face of America. Immigrants would still be given tests for health, intelligence, morality and security.

The force of this argument is recognized by the special measures enacted since 1952 which have ignored the established pattern of favoring Northern and Western Europe immigration over Southern and Eastern European countries. These statutes have resulted in the admission of a great many more persons from Southern European countries than would have been possible under the McCarran-Walter Act.

But more than a decade has elapsed since the last substantial amendment to these laws. There is a compelling need for Congress to re-examine and make changes in them.

Religious and civic organizations, ethnic associations and newspaper editorials, citizens from every walk of life and groups of every description have expressed their support for a more rational and less prejudiced immigration law. Congressional leaders of both parties have urged the adoption of new legislation that would eliminate the most objectionable features of the McCarran-Walter Act and the nationalities quota system.

It is not only the initial assignment of quota numbers which is arbitrary and unjust; additional inequity results from the failure of the law to permit full utilization of the

---

81 *irreconcilable* (adj.): that cannot be brought into harmony; unversöhnlich 82 *unrestricted* (adj.): not kept within limits 85 *sponsor* (v.): put forward a proposal 85/86 *status quo* (n.) /ˈsteɪtəsˋkwəʊ/: as it is now 87 *cosponsor* (v.): be a joint sponsor of a proposed piece of legislation 89 **clash** (n.): disagreement; conflict 90 **admission** (n.): being admitted 91 *proposal* (n.): s. th. proposed 93/94 *make over* (v.): change 95 *morality* (n.): good behaviour 97 *ignore* (v.): take no notice of 98 *statute* (n.) /ˋstætʃut/: (written) law passed by a law-making body 101 **decade** (n.) /ˋdekeɪd/: period of ten years 101 *elapse* (v.): (of time) pass 101 **substantial** (adj.): considerable 104 *civic* (adj.): of a city, citizens, or citizenship 104 **ethnic** (adj.): of a member of a minority or nationality group that is part of a larger community 104 *association* (n.): group of persons joined together for some common purpose 104 *editorial* (n.): special article or discussion of news in a newspaper, usu. written by the editor; Leitartikel 105 *walk of life* (n.): profession, occupation 105 *description* (n.): sort, kind 106 **rational** (adj.) /ˋræʃnl/: of reason or reasoning 106 **prejudiced** (adj.): biased; partial; voreingenommen, parteiisch 107 *urge* (v.): drive or force onward; incite 107 *adoption* (n.): acceptance 107 *eliminate* (v.): take or put away 108 *objectionable* (adj.): disagreeable; offensive 110 **initial** (adj.): of or at the beginning 110 *assignment* (n.): allotment; Zuordnung 110 *arbitrary* (adj.): willkürlich 111 *inequity* (n.): (instance of) injustice or unfairness 111 *utilization* (n.): making use of.

authorized quota numbers. The tiny principality of Andorra in the Pyrenees Mountains, with 6,500 Spanish-speaking inhabitants, has an American immigration quota of 100, while Spain, with 28 million people, has a quota of only 250. While American citizens wait for years for their relatives to receive a quota, approximately sixty thousand numbers are wasted each year because the countries to which they are assigned have far more numbers allocated to them than they have emigrants seeking to move to the United States. There is no way at present in which these numbers can be reassigned to nations where immense backlogs of applicants for admission to the United States have accumulated. This deficiency in the law should be corrected.

A special discriminatory formula is now applied to the immigration of persons who are attributable by their ancestry to an area called the Asia-Pacific triangle. This area embraces all countries from Pakistan to Japan and the Pacific islands north of Autralia and New Zealand. Usually, the quota under which a prospective immigrant

---

112 *authorize* (v.): give official approval to 112 *principality* (n.): Fürstentum 115 **approximately** (adv.): more or less exactly; ungefähr 117 *allocate* (v.): distribute or allot; zuordnen 119 *backlog* (n.): accumulation or reserve 119 *applicant* (n.): person who applies; Bewerber 120 **accumulate** (v.): become greater in number 120 *deficiency* (n.) /dɪˈfɪʃnsɪ/: state of being short of what is correct or needed 121 *formula* (n.) /ˈfɔmjʊlə/: Gesetzformel 122 *attributable* (adj.) /əˈtrɪbjutəbl/: to be thought of as belonging to 122 **ancestry** (n.): line of persons from whom one is descended 122 *triangle* (n.) /ˈtraɪæŋgl/: plane figure with three straight sides 124 *prospective* (adj.): expected or likely.

must enter is determined by his place of birth. However, if as much as one-half of an immigrant's ancestors came from nations in the Asia-Pacific triangle, he must rely upon the small quota assigned to the country of his ancestry, regardless of where he was born. This provision of the law should be repealed.

The Presidential message to Congress of July 23, 1963, recommended that the national origins system be replaced by a formula governing immigration to the United States which takes into account: (1) the skills of the immigrant and their relationships to our needs; (2) the family relationship between immigrants and persons already here, so that the reuniting of families is encouraged; and (3) the priority of registration. Present law grants a preference to immigrants with special skills, education or training. It also grants a preference to various relatives of the United States citizens and lawfully resident aliens. But it does so only within a national origins quota. It should be modified so that those with the greatest ability to add to the national welfare, no matter where they are born, are granted the highest priority. The next priority should go to those who seek to be reunited with their relatives. For applicants with equal claims, the earliest registrant should be the first admitted.

In order to remove other existing barriers to the reuniting of families, two additional improvements in the law are needed.

First, parents of American citizens, who now have a preferred quota status, should be accorded nonquota status.

Second, parents of aliens resident in the United States, who now have no preference, should be accorded a preference, after skilled specialists and other relatives of citizens and alien residents.

These changes will have little effect on the number of immigrants admitted. They will have a major effect insofar as they relieve the hardship many of our citizens and residents now face in being separated from their parents.

These changes will not solve all the problems of immigration. But they will insure that progress will continue to be made toward our ideals and toward the realization of humanitarian objectives.

We must avoid what the Irish poet John Boyle O'Reilly once called

Organized charity, scrimped and iced,
In the name of a cautious, statistical Christ.

Immigration policy should be generous; it should be fair; it should be flexible. With such a policy we can turn to the world, and to our own past, with clean hands and a clear conscience. Such a policy would be but a reaffirmation of old principles. It would

---

128 **repeal** (v.): revoke, cancel (a law) 131 *take into account*: consider; berücksichtigen 133 *priority* (n.) /praɪ`orətɪ/: s. th. given earlier attention 134 *registration* (n.): entering into a list 136 *alien* (n.) /`eɪlɪən/: foreigner 138 *welfare* (n.): well-being; prosperity 141 *barrier* (n.) /`bærɪə(r)/: Schranke 142 *improvement* (n.): betterment 144 *accord* (v.): grant 153 **objective** (n.) /əb`dʒektɪv/: s. th. aimed at 155 *scrimp* (v.): supply, use, less than enough of what is needed 159 *reaffirmation* (n.): affirming again.

be an expression of our agreement with George Washington that “The bosom of America is open to receive not only the opulent and respectable stranger, but the oppressed and persecuted of all nations and religions; whom we shall welcome to a participation of all our rights and privileges, if by decency and propriety of conduct they appear to merit the enjoyment.”

---

160 *bosom* (n.) /ˈbʊzəm/: (fig.) Busen 161 *opulent* (adj.): rich, wealthy 161 *respectable* (adj.): achtbar, anständig 162 *oppress* (v.): keep down by unjust or cruel government 162 **persecute** (v.): treat cruelly, esp. because of religious beliefs having or taking a share with others in some activity 163 *decency* (n.): respectable behaviour 163 *propriety* (n.): /prəˈpraɪətɪ/: state of being correct in behaviour and morals 163 *conduct* (n.): behaviour 164 *merit* (v.): deserve.

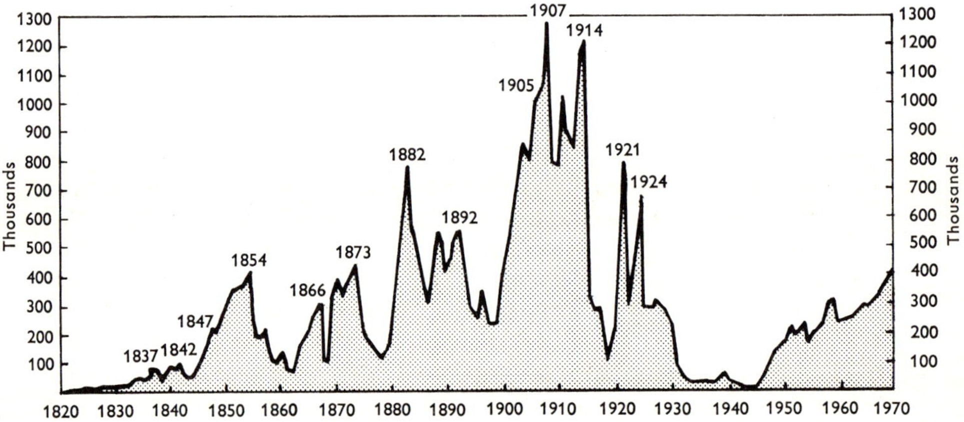

American immigration: 1820–1970

23: RICHARD VASQUEZ: Chicano

Chicano (1970) by Richard Vasquez is one of three major novels so far written by Chicano (Mexican-American) authors. (The other two are *Pocho* [1959] by José Antonio Villareal and *The Plum Pickers* [1969] by Raymond Barrio.)

The following text is from Richard Vasquez, *Chicano* (New York: Avon Books, 1971), pp. 34–41, 45–47.

[The Mexican Hector Sandoval, his wife Lita, their daughters Jilda and Hortensia, and their son Neftali one night pack up their things and leave their village for the United States. Though the immediate reason for their departure is the threat of Neftali's being pressed into the Mexican army, the ulterior motive for their emigration is their wish to flee from tyranny and poverty in Mexico. Before they leave, Hector says: "To los Estados Unidos. Where there will be no more of all that makes us suffer. Hurry now."]

The shrill, cold air knifed through his clothing to the flesh as Hector Sandoval drew the cowhide tighter around him and tensed his muscles, the more effectively to shiver. The railroad flatcar on which the family was riding bucketed along, swinging rhythmically, noisily nudging the car ahead, then impatiently tugging at the car behind. Jilda and Hortensia and their mother also lay flat, hides pulled around them. The last time Hector checked to see that they were bearing up under the ordeal they could hardly talk from the cold. Only Neftali sat, back to the wind, his cowhide encircling him and covering his head, but his face uncovered so that he could see. All yesterday and all night they had been riding. Dawn – and the sun – couldn't be far off. If there would be a sun. All Hector could make out of the sky was an uninterrupted overcast. He had expected California to be green country, soft pastures and farmlands, but so far he could only make out rugged, rocky hills, barren except for brush, cactus,

---

(Title) *Chicano* (n.) /tʃɪˈkɑnəʊ/: an American of Mexican or Latin American descent.

(Introduction) 1 **major** (adj.): more important

(Context) 4 *press* (v.): force a man to serve in the army or navy 4 *ulterior* (adj.) /ʌlˈtɪərɪə(r)/: beyond what is expressed or implied 5 **emigration** (n.): going from one's own country to another to settle there 5 **tyranny** (n.) /ˈtɪrənɪ/: cruel or unjust use of power 6 *los Estados Unidos* (n.): Spanish for the United States.

2 *cowhide* (n.): leather made from the hide of a cow 2 *tense* (v.): stiffen 2 *effective* (adj.): impressive 3 *flatcar* (n.): railroad car without a roof or sides, for carrying freight 3 *bucket* (v.): move or drive rapidly 4 *nudge* (v.): touch or push slightly 4 *tug* (v.): pull hard or violently 5 *hide* (n.): animal skin 6 *bear up* (v.): be strong in the face of sorrow, etc. 6 *ordeal* (n.): severe test of endurance; any painful experience 11 *overcast* (n.): cloud-covered sky 12 *rugged* (adj.) /ˈrʌgɪd/: rough, uneven 12 *barren* (adj.): (of land) not good enough to produce crops 12 *brush* (n.): rough low-growing bushes 12 *cactus* (n.): (sorts of) plant from hot, dry climates with a thick, fleshy stem, usu. with no leaves and covered with clusters of spines or prickles.

and an occasional group of stunted trees. …

He closed his eyes in the darkness and drew the hide tighter about him. …

He opened his eyes and saw that the sky was becoming light in the east. Odd, he thought, that merely the presence of light made the air feel warmer, more bearable, although he knew the sun couldn't possibly have warmed it yet.

The train slowed and as the wind decreased he felt warmer. Soon they were traveling not much faster than a man could walk, and he sat up and saw the others were sitting also, getting the first good look at their new country. He saw flat land, farmed and cultivated, as far as the eye could reach, with a backdrop of near-barren mountains. Farmhouses seemed spaced about a mile or so apart, and he was struck by their apparent affluence, evidenced by the accompanying auxiliary buildings such as storage facilities, barns, corrals and sheds.

A cold steady drizzle began to fall.

The Sandoval family was riding on one of half a hundred flatcars making up the train. Several other families also rode the train, and as it continued to slow they saw a trainman approaching, walking the length of each car, then leaping to the next. Hector watched as the man came to the car immediately ahead and said something to the family riding there. Then the man leaped onto the Sandoval car.

Hector was chilled by the look of complete and intentional disrespect the trainman gave him and his family. "You have to get off the train now," he said in broken Spanish, and kept walking toward the car to the rear.

"Can't we wait until the train stops?" Hector asked.

The man turned and, as though he hadn't heard, said in a loud voice, "If you don't get off now, you will all be very sorry," and he continued on.

Hector waited until a relatively even stretch of terrain came by and then, throwing off their belongings first, he jumped. Running alongside the train, he helped off first the children and then Lita, and the train kept going. The other families aboard the train chose to ride a little farther and risk the trainman's threat.

The Sandovals walked back and gathered their belongings, each carrying a fair share, and the caboose rolled noisily past. The sound of the train grew smaller and smaller and finally disappeared and as they stood looking about there was no sound at all, even the steady drizzle was silent.

A great sense of being alone in unfriendly territory gripped the family. The land was flat. A mile or more away, in opposite directions, were two farmhouses. A dog barked somewhere far off. The gray sky blended with the horizon. A hundred yards

---

13 *stunt* (v.): check or hinder the growth of 18 **decrease** (v.): become less 21 *backdrop* (n.): background 22 *space* (v.): arrange with spaces between 23 *affluence* (n.): wealth 23 **evidence** (v.): make clear; show proof 23 *auxiliary* (adj.): subsidiary; auxiliary building = Nebengebäude 24 *storage* (n.): space used for the storing of goods 24 *facilities* (pl. n.): Einrichtungen 24 *corral* (n.) /kə`ræl/: enclosure for horses or cattle 24 *shed* (n.): building used for storing things or for sheltering animals 25 *drizzle* (n.): fine rain 32 **intentional** (adj.): done on purpose 32 *disrespect* (n.): lack of respect; rudeness 38 *stretch* (n.): unbroken or continuous extent of country 38 *terrain* (n.) /tə`reɪn/: stretch of land, esp. with regard to its natural features 43 *caboose* (n.) /kə`bus/: AE small van at the end of a freight train for the use of the train men 48 *blend* (v.): mix together 48 *yard* (n.): 3 feet = 0,914 m 48 *tracks* (pl. n.): set of rails: Eisenbahnschienen.

from the tracks stood a grove of eucalyptus, and Hector saw a family camped by the stream that ran there. They approached the family to ask directions and share their fire, and were told the city was a dozen miles to the west. This family had also come by train, on the previous day, and were waiting only for a sick child to recover before pressing on to the city to look for work.

The Sandovals trudged on toward the city, laden with what possessions they had not traded or sold to get this far. By early afternoon they were entering the town, bone-weary, chilled and tired. The drizzle continued and the path beside the tracks veered and became a broad muddy road. Hector had seen many Mexicans working the fields nearby, but they had been reluctant to stop to talk to him.

The shacks were almost solid beside the road now, and an occasional store or business advertised its wares. Dios, Hector wondered aloud, was the whole city nothing but slum shacks and mud roads? He asked a man walking by. "No," the man smiled, "just the Mexican section."

A huge wagon loaded with produce came down the road, pulled by finer and larger horses than Hector had ever seen. The horses tugged mightily and the harness pressed into the shoulder flesh as the animals' strength fought to overcome the sluggish mud miring the wheels. The steady drizzle fell.

As they passed a row of shacks a woman came out and asked if they were new. She readily appointed herself their helper and showed them a brick shack next to her own. "This is vacant," she told Hector. "I think Señor Cárdenas will rent it to you. You have money?"

Hector reached into his pocket and felt the six dollars there. It was all he had after selling the burros and other things they could not carry when they left Trainwreck. It had been a much larger sum before he had converted it from pesos to dollars. "Yes, I have some."

"Good. Let the wife and children rest here with me. I'll feed them hot beans and soup. Go down this street to the cobblestone avenue, turn right, and in the tavern with the naked woman on the sign you'll find Cárdenas. Ask to rent this house. Then I'll tell you how to find work in this hell-hole."

Hector walked in the drizzle down the street. Mud squeezed through the holes in his shoes and made his feet hurt. His wide sombrero dripped water in front of his

---

49 *grove* (n.) /grəʊv/: small wood 49 *eucalyptus* (n.) /ˈjukəˋlɪptəs/: (sort of) tall evergreen tree from which an oil, used for colds, is obtained 51 *mile* (n.): 1,609 km 53 *press on* (v.): continue in a determined way 54 *trudge* (v.): walk wearily or heavily 54 *laden* (adj.): loaded, burdened 55 *trade* (v.): exchange 56 *bone-weary* (adj.): knochenmüde 57 *veer* (v.): turn around to change in direction 57 *muddy* (adj.): full of, covered with, mud 58 **reluctant** (adj.): unwilling, disinclined 59 *shack* (n.): small, roughly built shed, hut or house 60 *Dios* (interj.): Spanish for God 63 *produce* (n.) /ˋprodjus/: s. th. produced, esp. fruit or vegetables 64 *harness* (n.) /ˋhɑnɪs/: all the leather-work and metal-work by which a horse is controlled and fastened to a cart, etc. 65 *sluggish* (adj.): inactive, slow-moving 66 *mire* (v.): cover with mud 68 **appoint** (v.): choose for a post 69 *vacant* (adj.) /ˋveɪkənt/: not occupied by anyone 69 *rent* (v.): allow to be used or occupied in return for regular payment 72 *burro* (n.) /ˋbʊrəʊ/: Spanish for donkey 72 *Trainwreck*: the village in Mexico where the Sandovals come from 73 *convert* (v.): (in eine andere Währung) umrechnen 73 *peso* (n.) /ˋpeɪsəʊ/: unit of currency in many Latin American countries 76 *cobblestone* (n.): Pflasterstein 76 *tavern* (n.): saloon, bar; inn 79 *squeeze through* (v.): (sich) hindurchquetschen 80 *sombrero* (n.) /somˋbreərəʊ/: a broad-brimmed, tall-crowned felt or straw hat of a kind worn in Mexico and the Southwest of the U. S.

face whenever he tipped his head forward. He wore the cowhide around his shoulders like a sarape and was reasonably dry down to his knees.

The structures lining the streets were primarily living quarters. Ragged children, noses hanging mucus, barefoot in the mud, played in the street or shrieked in the shacks. Groups of men stood around at corners and on the dirt walks, talking. Some wore clothing in shreds, were unshaven and barefoot. Hector noticed a great variety of attire, but poverty was the common style. He talked with a few persons and discovered that finding work in the fields and orchards was on the minds of all. Everyone, it seemed, was almost starving, and "until more crops are ready" was the universal phrase, the thought that gave all here the determination to remain in the barrio bajo.

All the shacks, the tiny stores and businesses lining the streets for blocks in all directions had been erected, Hector saw, on a purely temporary basis, to make do, to improvise until something more substantial could be built, but all the temporary shelters and shops had become a town, a town for people who lived in anticipation of the time when "more crops are ready," and it was a town such as Hector had never heard of.

The street he was now on was the main street. He stopped at a corner and looked around. The drizzle still fell, making little rivulets on the street, which the children tried to dam up or channel. Diagonally from where he stood was a tavern, the walls of which were galvanized sheet metal. The front was open, as the large door was hinged at the top and swung upward. It was tied in place so that it afforded a little shelter to a group of men, dressed like tramps, who swore loudly in Spanish and passed a bottle among themselves. He was about to cross the street when he heard hoofs splashing in the mud.

He noticed heads turning and saw two men approaching on horseback. As they came closer he saw that they were americanos and wore badges. He noted that their horses were magnificent, well fed, large and muscular, well trained. The saddles were of rich leather, and the men wore soft hats, riding boots, and huge pistols at the hip.

---

81 *tip* (v.): lean or tilt on one side 82 *sarape* (n.) /sə`rɑˈpi/: Mexican-Spanish for a woollen blanket, often brightly coloured, used as an outer garment by men in Latin American countries 83 *ragged* (adj.) /`rægɪd/: badly torn or in rags 84 *mucus* (n.) /`mjukəs/: sticky, slimy substance produced within the nose 86 *shred* (n.): strip or piece torn off s. th. 87 *attire* (n.) /ə`tɑɪə(r)/: (lit. or poet.) dress 89 *crop* (n.) any agricultural product, growing or harvested 91 *barrio bajo* (n.) /`bʌrɪəʊˈbʌkhəʊ/: Spanish for lower section of a town; in this context the term means Mexican-American ghetto 93 **temporary** (adj.): designed to be used for a short time only 93 *basis* (n.) /`beɪsɪs/: Basis, Grundlage 93 *make do* (v.): answer a need; auskommen, sich begnügen 94 **substantial** (adj.): solidly or strongly built or made 95 *anticipation* (n.): hope 99 *rivulet* (n.) /`rɪvjʊlət/: small stream 100 *dam up* (v.): hold back by means of a barrier 100 *channel* (v.): cause to go through a channel 100 *diagonal* (adj.) /dɑɪ`ægənl/: (straight line) going across a straight-sided figure 101 *galvanize* (v.): coat (sheet iron, etc.) with metal 101 *sheet metal* (n.): Metallblech 102 *hinge* (v.): attach with a joint on which a door turns or swings 103 *swear* (v.): use curses and profane language 105 *hoof* (n.): horny part of the foot of a horse: Huf 105 *splash* (v.): cause a liquid to fly about in drops 107 *americano* (n.) /ʌməri`kɑnəʊ/: Spanish for American 107 *badge* (n.): piece of metal worn on a uniform to show a person's rank 108 *magnificent* (adj.) /mæg`nɪfɪsnt/: splendid.

Their horses were coming at a casual trot. As they neared, one rider suddenly spurred his mount ahead and rode to the rear entrance of the tavern Hector had noticed. The other rider spurred to the front door. The men who had been in front scattered.

Except for the men on the train, this was Hector's first look at americanos. He noticed the lawmen were stern, fierce and unflinching.

From his vantage point Hector could see the rider sitting on his mount facing the rear door of the tavern, and the other now dismounted and, feeling reassuringly for his pistol, quickly walked inside. Hector heard a few loud shouts, then something he couldn't understand in English. He couldn't see the man inside, but the door at the rear burst open and a young tattered man, bearded and wearing a sombrero, ran out, obviously fleeing. He took only a few steps before he saw the mounted man in front of him. He stopped just as the rider drew his pistol and fired. The tattered man clutched his breast and swayed, and the rider took careful aim and fired again. The man collapsed. The lawman rode up to the fallen man and, pointing his pistol almost directly down, put another bullet into the still form.

The other lawman came out the rear door, examined the body briefly, went to his mount and the pair rode off at a casual trot.

Hector joined the gathering crowd at the rear of the tavern. All looked down at the dead man. "He shouldn't have tried to run" . . . "Never run from a gringo policeman" . . . "They wanted to question him about the knife fight he had in the americano town the other night" . . . "He was a bad one" . . . "They had him in jail before and they let him go."

A young woman appeared, carrying an infant perhaps six months old and holding the hand of another child of three. Hector knew immediately, when the crowd quieted and parted to let her through, that she was the widow. She stood a long moment looking down at her dead husband, her eyes streaming, more with pity than grief, Hector thought. The infant stirred and his face sought her breast. She untied a drawstring on her blouse and, while one hand wiped away tears the hand of the arm cradling the baby guided his head to her nipple, as though she had practiced these movements.

Her other son standing beside her pulled at her skirt.

"Mama! Is Papa dead? Mama! Answer me. Is Papa dead?"

---

110 **casual** (adj.) /ˈkæʒʊəl/: informal; lässig 110 *trot* (n.): (of horses, etc.) going at a pace faster than a walk but not so fast as a gallop 110 *spur* (v.): urge on with spurs (= Sporen) 111 *mount* (n.): horse 111 rear (adj): of, at, or in the back part 112 *scatter* (v.): go in different directions 114 *lawman* (n.): law officer, esp. a marshal or sheriff 114 *stern* (adj.): demanding and enforcing obedience 114 *unflinching* (adj.): fearless, resolute 115 *vantage point* (n.): position allowing a clear view 116 *dismount* (v.): get down from a horse 116 *reassure* (v.) /ˌriəˈʃʊə(r)/: remove the fears or doubts of; (sich) vergewissern 119 *tattered* (adj.): zerlumpt 122 *clutch* (v.): grasp tightly 122 *sway* (v.): move first to one side and then to the other 123 *collapse* (v.): fall down 125 *out* (prep.): AE for BE out of 128 *gringo* (n.): in Latin America, a hostile and contemptuous term for a foreigner, esp. an American 129 *question* (v.): (legal use) ask questions of 133 *quiet* (v.): become quiet 135 *stream* (v.): flow freely 136 **infant** (n.): child during the first years of its life 137 *drawstring* (n.): string that tightens a blouse, etc. 138 *cradle* (v.): hold in or as in a cradle (= Wiege) 138 *nipple* (n.): part of the breast through which a baby gets its mother's milk.

Chicano agricultural workers show their identification papers to border patrolmen.

A heavy elderly woman wearing a dress that came to her ankles came forward and disengaged the child's hand from his mother. "Yes, little one, your papa is dead. Now come with me. Your mother needs to cry and you'll bother her. We'll go to my house."

"Do you have any more chicken like you had last time?" the boy asked.

"We'll see. I'll give you something good to eat, I promise."

"All I want?"

The old woman led the boy away. The young mother stood looking down at her husband's corpse, her baby suckling half-heartedly. She looked up, and Hector saw her thin beauty and grace.

"Who will help me bury him?" she asked. A half dozen men stepped forth reluctantly, some complaining the dead man still owed them money or favors, all taking in the slender body and full buttocks and breasts. Hector turned to go, knowing that when a girl like this was widowed, she usually ended up better off than before, and he suspected this would be the case.

By the time he got to the tavern with the large painting of a nude woman on the front (the tavern was called The Naked Woman), word of the shooting had spread. It was on everyone's lips as he entered.

Catching his eyes first as he looked around were the young girls, gaudily dressed, sitting provocatively on a bench against the rear wall as though they were on display.

---

142 *ankle* (n.): joint connecting the foot with the leg 143 *disengage* (v.): separate 144 **bother** (v.) /AE `bʌðə(r); BE `boðə(r)/: worry, trouble, harass 149 **corpse** (n.): dead body 149 *suckle* (v.): feed at the breast 149 *half-hearted* (adj.): with little enthusiasm or interest 153 *take in* (v.): watch with excitement 153 *buttock* (n.) /`bʌtək/: either side of that part of the body on which a person sits 159 *gaudy* (adj.): bright and showy, but in bad taste 160 *provocative* (adj.) /prə`vokətɪv/: provoking desire.

There were nearly a dozen and some appeared to be scarcely into their teens. It had been many years since he had seen working prostitutes and their youthfulness shocked him. His own girls were older, he realized.

Ten or twelve men were at the bar drinking, and a like number were scattered throughout, drinking at tables or trying to tease the young prostitutes.

Hector ordered a mug of beer at the bar and observed. A fat man, as fat as himself and about the same age, was seated at a table near the girls. The others nearby were enjoying the conversation between the fat one and one of the girls.

"Fifty cents! For one time! That's too much."

"Nobody's begging you."

"Besides, my wife and kids need the money for food."

"Then go home to your wife."

"Now, if you would just trust me, until the Valencia crop starts next week . . ."

"Sure I trust you until next week. Come back then. You can trust I'll be here."

Laughter from the spectators.

"I don't think you're worth fifty cents."

"You'll never know until you try, will you?"

"But you're so young. You probably don't know how to screw very well."

"It'll cost you fifty cents to find out."

"Aw, come on. I can spare twenty-five cents."

She shook her head smartly. "I'm worth fifty. Ask your amigo over there."

"Where? Who? You mean Paco? Paco! Tell me, is the little lady worth fifty cents?"

"Dios! That little lady is worth fifty dollars!"

Laughter again echoed.

Hector turned his attention to the man behind the bar.

"I'm looking for a man called Cárdenas."

"It's me."

"I want to rent the place by the bakery there. It's empty."

The man showed interest. "Fine. Three dollars a month. Pay me now for the first month. There's a water pipe running inside, and I just had a new toilet dug out in back. It's got a stove, too."

Hector gave the man three dollars and Cárdenas took a pencil and paper. He made a note of the transaction and gave Hector a slip showing \$ 3 received. The business transacted, Cárdenas moved away to wait on customers.

Hector finished his mug of beer and ordered another. Then a swell of applause burst out. Looking to the rear, Hector saw that the fat man and the young girl had finally struck a bargain and were going through the door to the side. All cheered or clapped and returned to their drinking.

---

162 *prostitute* (n.): person who offers herself for sexual intercourse for payment 165 **tease** (v.): annoy by mocking, poking fun, etc. 166 *mug* (n.): as much as a mug (= Bierkrug) will hold; ein „großes" Glas (Bier) 173 *Valencia*: special kind of orange 178 screw (v.): (taboo) have sexual intercourse with 180 *spare* (v.): afford to give money for s. th. 181 *smart* (adj.): clever; lively 181 *amigo* (n.) /ʌ`migəʊ/: Spanish for friend 188 *bakery* (n.): place where bread is baked 190 *pipe* (n.): tube through which liquids or gases can flow 190/191 *in back* (*of*): AE prep. for behind, at the rear of 193 *transaction* (n.): piece of business 195 *swell* (n.): gradual increase in the volume of sound 197 *strike a bargain*: conclude a bargain.

Hector struck up conversation with two men standing by. He learned this place was the starting point. Immigrants and U.S.-born migrant workers came here – at least a large number did – each year and began spreading out eastward and northward. This was a coastal city, and they told him there was a thousand miles of crops to be picked north and east. But things were tough. It took money to live, and to get from one place to another. So you had to work around here for a month or two, so you could buy shoes and clothes and transportation. And there were too many Mexicans here. Without luck, you could go a month or two looking for work.

Hector noticed an American come in. He was nattily dressed and in a hurry. He motioned to Cárdenas and the bar owner approached. Although Hector didn't try, he couldn't help hearing.

"I need four right now. Party. Guarantee two dollars each."

Cárdenas beckoned and his girls came to him. "Americano party. Go with him. Nothing doing here. I want my usual cut."

The girls perked up with enthusiasm at the mention of Americano party, and followed the gringo out.

[Hector goes back to his new house. The next morning he starts out to look for work.]

He started out. A few blocks away he passed the waiting place. At least a hundred and fifty men were gathered at a corner. Some were literally in rags. Some wore the white pajama-type work clothes of the Mexican peasant. Some wore American clothes. Most wore hats, and there were many sombreros among them, and all had large mustachios and talked in Spanish.

It was still cold and drizzling, and the waiting men joked little. Doña Dora had warned him not to hang out here, and he was not enough at home to take the responsibility of going against advice. But he walked slowly past. The main body of men stood on a corner, watching an approaching wagon. They crowded to the fore. Hector saw a small, slight man who looked almost feverish. He was trying to slip in at the front. Someone roughly shoved him back.

"Please," the little man pleaded. "My family, they are actually starving. I've got to work soon." He addressed one nice-looking young man. "Just let me stand here near the front."

"Sure," the man said, "just so you don't stand in front of me," and he firmly pushed the little man back. A large, fierce-looking man shoved him farther back, and yet another man said, "Don't get in front of me. I want to work, too."

---

200 **immigrant** (n.): person who comes into another country to settle there.
200 *migrant worker* (n.) /`maɪgrənt/: farm labourer who moves from place to place to harvest seasonal crops 203 *take* (v.): need; require 205 *transportation* (n.): fare or a ticket for being transported 207 *natty* (adj.): trim and stylish 211 *beckon* (v.) /`bekən/: call s. b.'s attention by a movement of the hand or arm, usu. to show that he is to come nearer or to follow 212 *cut* (n.): AE sl. for share; Anteil 213 *perk up* (v.): become lively and active 217 *literally* (adv.): buchstäblich 220 *mustachio* (n.) /mʊs`tʌtʃəʊ/: (from Spanish mostacho or Italian mostaccio) mustache, esp. a large, bushy one 222 *hang out* (v.): AE sl. for spend much time 224 *to the fore*: to the front 225 *slight* (adj.): slim, frail-looking 226 *shove* (v.) /ʃʌv/: push 230 *just so*: provided that as long as.

The wagon pulled up, and like an ocean wave, the men moved in on it. An American driving the team stood up.

"Twenty, that's all, twenty. A dollar and a half for the day, if you work hard." He counted out twenty as they scrambled on the wagon and then cracked the horses' rumps with a wide leather strap and the wagon lurched through the mud. The remaining men went back to pushing and shoving to get a better position for the next wagon. Those at the rear, with no hope of getting on the next wagon, found seats and argued or passed bottles back and forth.

Hector walked on.

At the farm he found the foreman striding among the orange trees, a notebook in his hand as he kept track of each worker's output. "You're in luck," he told Hector in broken Spanish. "We've got to rush to finish the navel crop. It was late. And the Valencias will be ready next month. Get in there and start stripping that row. Keep up with the others and you got a job." A tired but happy Hector trudged home in the evening to break the good news to his family.

---

236 *scramble* (v.): climb 236 *crack* (v.): (coll.) hit hard 237 *rump* (n.): animal's buttocks 237 *strap* (n.): narrow strip of leather 237 *lurch* (v.): move along with a sudden change of weight to one side 243 *keep track of*: keep an account or; stay informed about 243 *output* (n.): work done, esp. over a given period 244 *navel crop* (n.): harvesting a special kind of oranges 245 *strip* (v.): pluck so as to make empty 247 *break the news to s. b.*: tell s. b. the news.

24: PIRI THOMAS: Alien Turf

Piri Thomas (1928–) spent his early childhood in Manhattan's Spanish Harlem during the depression years. A black Puerto Rican, he was constantly torn by his search for identity between different cultures.

The following text is from Piri Thomas' autobiography *Down These Mean Streets* (New York: Vintage Books, 1974, pp. 26–30), which was first published in 1967.

Sometimes you don't fit in. Like if you're a Puerto Rican on an Italian block. After my new baby brother, Ricardo, died of some kind of germs, Poppa moved us from 111th Street to Italian turf on 114th Street between Second and Third Avenue. I guess Poppa wanted to get Momma away from the hard memories of the old pad.

I sure missed 111th Street, where everybody acted, walked, and talked like me. But on 114th Street everything went all right for a while. There were a few dirty looks from the spaghetti-an'-sauce cats, but no big sweat. Till that one day I was on my way home from school and almost had reached my stoop when someone called: "Hey, you dirty fuckin' spic."

The words hit my ears and almost made me curse Poppa at the same time. I turned around real slow and found my face pushing in the finger of an Italian kid about my age. He had five or six of his friends with him.

"Hey, you," he said. "What nationality are ya?"

I looked at him and wondered which nationality to pick. And one of his friends said, "Ah, Rocky, he's black enuff to be a nigger. Ain't that what you is, kid?"

My voice was almost shy in its anger. "I'm Puerto Rican," I said. "I was born here." I wanted to shout it, but it came out like a whisper.

"Right here inna street?" Rocky sneered. "Ya mean right here inna middle of da street?"

They all laughed.

(Title) **alien** (adj.) /ˈeɪlɪən/: foreign *turf* (n.): AE sl. for a neighborhood area regarded by a street gang as its own territory to be defended against other gangs.

(Introduction) 1/2 *Spanish Harlem:* quarter in Upper Manhattan inhabited by Spanish-speaking people 2 **depression** (n.): period of reduced business, much unemployment, etc. 3 *torn between*: painfully distracted by having to choose between conflicting demands, wishes, etc.

2 *block* (n.): Häuserblock 2 *germs* (pl. n.): Bazillen 2 *Poppa* (n.) /ˈpʌpə/: AE familiar for daddy 5 *pad* (n.): AE sl. for the place where one lives; Wohnung 6 *I sure missed*: AE coll. for I surely missed 8 *cat* (n.): AE sl. for any person, esp. a man; Typ 8 *no big sweat*: AE sl. for no trouble or difficulty at all 9 *stoop* (n.): small covered entrance at the door of a house 10 *fuckin'* (adj.): (taboo) damned 10 *spic* (n.): AE derog. for an American of Spanish ancestry; hence a Puerto Rican 12 *slow*: AE coll. for slowly 12 *kid* (n.): AE coll. for a young person 19 *sneer* (v.): show contempt by means of a derisive smile; utter contemptuous words.

I hated them. I shook my head slowly from side to side. "Uh-uh," I said softly. "I was born inna hospital – inna bed."

"Umm, *paisan* – born inna bed," Rocky said.

I didn't like Rocky Italiano's voice. "Inna hospital," I whispered, and all the time my eyes were trying to cut down the long distance from this trouble to my stoop. But it was no good; I was hemmed in by Rocky's friends. I couldn't help thinking about kids getting wasted for moving into a block belonging to other people.

"What hospital, *paisan?*" Bad Rocky pushed.

"Harlem Hospital," I answered, wishing like all hell that it was 5 o'clock, instead of just 3 o'clock, 'cause Poppa came home at 5. I looked around for some friendly faces belonging to grown-up people, but the elders were all busy yakking away in Italian. I couldn't help thinking how much like Spanish it sounded. Shit, that should make us something like relatives.

"Harlem Hospital?" said a voice. "I knew he was a nigger."

"Yeah," said another voice from an expert on color. "That's the hospital where all them black bastards get born at."

I dug three Italian elders looking at us from across the street, and I felt saved. But that went out the window when they just smiled and went on talking. I couldn't decide whether they had smiled because this new whatever-he-was was gonna get his ass kicked or because they were pleased that their kids were welcoming a new kid to their country. An older man nodded his head at Rocky, who smiled back. I wondered if that was a signal for my funeral to begin.

"Ain't that right, kid?" Rocky pressed. "Ain't that where all black people get born?"

I dug some of Rocky's boys grinding and pushing and punching closed fists against open hands. I figured they were looking to shake me up, so I straightened up my humble voice and made like proud. "There's all kinds of people born there. Colored people, Puerto Ricans like me, an' – even spaghetti-benders like you."

"That's a dirty fuckin' lie" – *bash,* I felt Rocky's fist smack into my mouth – "you dirty fuckin' spic."

I got dizzy and then more dizzy when fists started to fly from everywhere and only toward me. I swung back, *splat, bish* – my fist hit some face and I wished I hadn't, 'cause then I started getting kicked.

I heard people yelling in Italian and English and I wondered if maybe it was 'cause I hadn't fought fair in having hit that one guy. But it wasn't. The voices were trying to help me.

---

22 *uh–uh* (interj.) /ˋəˈə/: an exclamation indicating a negative response 24 *paisan* (n.) /ˈpɑɪˋsʌn/: AE sl. for comrade, pal; also paisano 27 *hem in* (v.): surround 28 *get wasted* (v.): get destroyed 32 *yak* (v.): AE sl. for talk much or idly 33 *shit* (interj.): (taboo) an expression of strong disgust or disappointment 38 *dig* (v.): AE sl. for notice, see, look at, or identify someone 41 *ass* (n.) /æs/: AE taboo for the behind; Hintern 43 *funeral* (n.): burial; Beerdigung 46 *grind* (v.): AE sl. for move one's body 46 *punch* (v.): strike hard with the fist 47 *figure* (v.) /ˋfɪgjər/: AE coll. for believe, think, consider 47 *shake up* (v.): AE sl. for beat up 48 *make like* (v.): AE sl. for pretend to be, behave or act in a specific manner 49 *spaghetti-bender* (n.): (derog.) an Italian 50 *bash* (v.): (echoic) hit hard 50 *smack* (adv.): AE coll. for directly; precisely 52 *dizzy* (adj.): feeling as if everything were turning around, as if unable to balance; schwindelig 53 *splat* (interj.): a slapping sound 53 *bish* (interj.): same as bash; hit hard 55 *yell* (v.): cry out loudly; scream.

"Whas'sa matta, you no-good kids, leeva da kid alone," a man said. I looked through a swelling eye and dug some Italians pushing their kids off me with slaps. One even kicked a kid in the ass. I could have loved them if I didn't hate them so fuckin' much.

"You all right, kiddo?" asked the man.

"Where you live, boy?" said another one.

"Is the *bambino* hurt?" asked a woman.

I didn't look at any of them. I felt dizzy. I didn't want to open my mouth to talk, 'cause I was fighting to keep from puking up. I just hoped my face was cool-looking. I walked away from that group of strangers. I reached my stoop and started to climb the steps.

"Hey, spic," came a shout from across the street. I started to turn to the voice and changed my mind. "Spic" wasn't my name. I knew that voice, though. It was Rocky's. "We'll see ya again, spic," he said.

---

59 *slap* (n.): hard hit 62 *kiddo* (n.) /ˋkɪdəʊ/: AE sl. for kid (= young person); in AE sl. the suffix -o gives the word a familiar or flippant connotation 64 *bambino* (n.) /ˈbʌmˋbinɔ/: Italian for child 66 *puke up* (v.): (coll.) vomit, throw up; kotzen.

I wanted to do something tough, like spitting in their direction. But you gotta have spit in your mouth in order to spit, and my mouth was hurt dry. I just stood there with my back to them.

"Hey, your old man just better be the janitor in that fuckin' building."

Another voiced added, "Hey, you got any pretty sisters? We might let ya stay onna block."

Another voice mocked. "Aw, fer Chrissake, where ya ever hear of one of them black broads being pretty?"

I heard the laughter. I turned around and looked at them. Rocky made some kind of dirty sign by putting his left hand in the crook of his right arm while twisting his closed fist in the air.

Another voice said, "Fuck it, we'll just cover the bitch's face with the flag an' fuck er for old glory."

All I could think of was how I'd like to kill each of them two or three times. I found some spit in my mouth and splattered it in their direction and went inside.

Momma was cooking, and the smell of rice and beans was beating the smell of Parmesan cheese from the other apartments. I let myself into our new pad. I tried to walk fast past Momma so I could wash up, but she saw me.

"My God, Piri, what happened?" she cried.

"Just a little fight in school, Momma. You know how it is, Momma, I'm new in school an' . . ." I made myself laugh. Then I made myself say, "But Moms, I whipped the living — outta two guys, an' one was bigger'n me."

"Bendito, Piri, I raise this family in Christian way. Not to fight. Christ says to turn the other cheek."

"Sure, Momma." I smiled and went and showered, feeling sore at Poppa for bringing us into spaghetti country. I felt my face with easy fingers and thought about all the running back and forth from school that was in store for me.

I sat down to dinner and listened to Momma talk about Christian living without really hearing her. All I could think of was that I hadda go out in that street again. I made up my mind to go out right after I finished eating. I had to, shook up or not; cats like me had to show heart.

---

75 *janitor* (n.) /ˈdʒænɪtə/: AE one who takes care of a building; Hausmeister 78 *fer Chrissake* (interj.) /ˈkraɪsˈseɪk/: AE coll. for damned; for Christ's sake 79 *broad* (n.): AE sl. for a woman or girl 81 *crook* (n.): bend; Krümmung 83 *fuck it* (interj.): (taboo) an expression of dismay or annoyance 83 *bitch* (n.): AE sl. for a woman or prostitute 84 *old glory* (n.): the flag of the U. S. 86 *splatter* (v.): spatter or plash; (be)spritzen 87 *Momma* (n.) /ˈmʌmə/: AE familiar for mother 93 the living ———: (taboo) the living shit 94 *bendito* (adj.) Spanish for blessed 96 *sore at* (adj.): AE for angry with 98 *be in store for s. b.*: await one in the future 101 *shook up* (adj.): AE sl. for upset; agitated 102 *show heart*: show courage.

25: WILLIAM ALBERT ALLARD: Chinatown, the Gilded Ghetto

The following article is from *National Geographic,* Vol. 148, No. 5 (November 1975), pp. 630–34, 639.

One Step Away From Citizenship

Richard Chung, 71, came to America 54 years ago. For much of that time he lived here illegally. Richard has a happy face. His smile comes on like an explosion.

"When I 16, I work on British ship that sails to San Francisco," he told me. "I jump ship with 40 other men. That was when Chinese not allowed to immigrate to America. I keep moving, working as janitor and on farms, and up in Alaska in salmon-canning factories. But all the time, I can't walk the streets, I can't go anywhere. I much afraid. When I 19, I work in restaurant owned by Chinese lady. She tell me go to school. So I enroll and go to school four years."

For several decades, Richard saved his money to make a trip back to China. But as an illegal alien, he lacked the papers that would allow him to leave the U. S. and return. So he bought *kah-gee,* false papers.

When the San Francisco earthquake and fire in 1906 destroyed public records, a new kind of American was created: the "paper citizen," who claimed to have been born in San Francisco and appeared in court with documents to support the claim.

"I pay four hundred dollars for papers," Richard said, "made by a friend with an old typewriter and old paper. But when it comes time to apply for passport, I still afraid."

It took a war to make Richard a citizen. In the mid-1940's, as a gesture to an ally, the U. S. repealed Chinese exclusion legislation and permitted those who were already here legally to apply for citizenship.

(Title) *Chinatown* (n.): the Chinese quarter of any city outside of China *gild* (v.): make s. th. seem more attractive or more valuable than it is; (fig.) overlay with a thin layer of gold *ghetto* (n.): any section of a city in which members of a minority group live.

1 **citizenship** (n.): having the full rights of a citizen 3 *illegally* (adv.): not legally 3 *explosion* (n.): outburst or outbreak 4/5 *jump ship*: leave a ship illegally 5 **immigrate** (v.): come into another country in order to settle there 6 *janitor* (n.) /ˈdʒænɪtə(r)/: AE person hired to take care of a building; Hausmeister 6 *salmon* (n.) /ˈsæmən/: large fish, valued for food and the sport of catching it with rod and line; Lachs 6 *salmon-canning* (n.): putting salmon up in cans or jars for preservation 9 *enroll* (v.): become a member (of a school, etc.) 10 **decade** (n.) /ˈdekeɪd/: period of ten years 11 **alien** (n.) /ˈeɪlɪən/: foreigner who is not a citizen of the country in which he is 13 *earthquake* (n.): sudden, violent movements of the earth's surface 13 *record* (n.): written account of facts etc. 17 *typewriter* (n.): Schreibmaschine 19 **gesture** (n.) /ˈdʒestʃə(r)/: an act made merely for an effect; Geste 19 *ally* (n.) /ˈælaɪ/: country joined with another for a common purpose 20 **repeal** (v.): revoke, annul (a law, etc.); aufheben 20 **exclusion** (n.): refusal to admit (a person, group of persons) as an immigrant or as immigrants 20 **legislation** (n.) /ˌledʒɪsˈleɪʃn/: Gesetzgebung 21 **apply for** (v.): (formally) ask for; sich bewerben um.

A Street in San Francisco's Chinatown

"I take all my money out of bank," Richard recalled, "war bonds, everything, because I know they send me home. But they don't! They let me stay because I tell the truth. Lucky I go to school!"

How different things are today – when the Chinese in San Francisco have taken a strong position against busing school children to achieve racial balance in the classroom. One chief reason: The long ride would take from the children the time they spend learning the Chinese language. Like other minorities, many Chinese believe the best way to reap America's promise of opportunity is to remain distinctly and proudly ethnic, even though with an American accent.

In 1965 all reference to race was eliminated in determining immigration status. Each nation outside the Western Hemisphere got a quota of 20,000 immigrants annually. America's door was open again to Chinese.

But for many of the 4,000 or so immigrants who now arrive annually in San Francisco, the going can be rough. Jobs are few and pay little. Newcomers with limited knowledge of English cannot qualify for work elsewhere in the city. A college graduate from Hong Kong who can't speak much English will probably start life here as a dishwasher.

On a beautiful San Francisco evening, I called on the family of Jack Leong, who had just a four-bedroom apartment in a barracks-like housing project, Ping Yuen, on Pacific Avenue. In 1969 the Leongs came to Chinatown from Hong Kong, where all the children except the baby had been born. Jack Leong was unemployed. I brought a bag of oranges for the children. If I offered to give them anything else, the parents might be offended.

They were just finishing dinner in the sparsely furnished but clean apartment, and I joined them at the kitchen table for a cup of tea. Jack and his wife, Yuet, did not speak English, so Mary, the oldest of five children, spoke for the family. The others were shy, silent, watchful. I asked Mary why they had come to Chinatown, where life seemed so filled with obstacles.

"It's really better here than in Hong Kong," she said. "It's so crowded there, and jobs are even harder to find than in Chinatown. My parents are like most Chinese; they want their children to get a good education.

---

22 *war bond* (n.): printed paper issued by a government acknowledging that money has been lent to it and will be paid back with interest 26 *position* (n.): attitude; opinion 26 *busing* (n.): (also bussing) transporting children by bus from Chinatown to schools in white areas and vice versa to achieve racial integration 26 **achieve** (v.): gain or reach by effort 26 *racial* (adj.) /ˈreɪʃl/: relating to race 28 **minority** (n.) /maɪˈnorətɪ; AE also mɪˈnɔrətɪ/: a racial, religious or political group that differs from the larger, controlling group 30 **ethnic** (adj.): of race 31 *reference* (n.): Bezug, Hinweis 31 *eliminate* (v.): omit; remove 31 *status* (n.) /ˈsteɪtəs/: person's legal position in relation to others 32 *the Western Hemisphere*: the American continent; cf. text 2, line 56 32 **quota** (n.): limited number of immigrants allowed to enter a country 35 *going* (n.): AE sl. work; circumstances under which one has to make a living 35 *newcomer* (n.): person who has recently arrived in a place 36 *elsewhere* (adv.): in some other place, somewhere else 37 *graduate* (n.) /ˈgrædʒʊət/: one who has completed a course at an educational institution 40 *barracks-like* (adj.): kasernengleich 40 *housing project* (n.) /ˈhaʊzɪŋ ˈprɔdʒəkt/: AE complex of inexpensive apartments or houses, esp. one that is publicly owned or financed 45 *sparsely* (adv.) /ˈspɑslɪ/: thinly spread 45 *furnish* (v.): put furniture in 48 *watchful* (adj.): watching closely; vigilant; alert 49 **obstacle** (n.): s. th. in the way that stops progress or makes it difficult.

"It is hard to find a good place to live here," she continued. "We waited four years for this apartment. It's the largest kind they have in the housing projects, and they are much in demand. But before we moved here, we had only one room, so it's much nicer now."

As Mary spoke, the other children hovered near me, not quite sure how close they dared come. Nine-year-old May, a chief of absolute beauty, was at my side and for just a moment her fingers grazed mine, then pulled back.

Mary said her father had been a cook in one of Chinatown's restaurants, where he made about $500 a month, working ten hours a day, six days a weeek. But a leg injury now had him looking for a job that would not require him to stand for such long periods.

"Needed to Run Sewing Machines"

Mrs. Leong sewed at home for a garment maker. Before the baby came, she sewed wedding dresses for 30 cents an hour. Her face brightened when Mary talked about the "so many nice people" who had helped them.

"And my English is getting better because my schoolteachers and the other children all helped me to learn." She repeated this to her parents in Chinese. Her mother responded with the old gesture of thumbs up.

Yee yan cher yee is a phrase frequently seen in help-wanted ads in Chinatown's newspapers. It means "people needed to operate sewing machines." Often the only work women can find is in one-room garment-factory sweatshops, of which some 150 are scattered through Chinatown. They sew bathing suits, shirts, dresses, and other garments at piece rates.

Although they pay less than $1 an hour, far below the federal minimum of $2.10, the sweatshops offer one advantage: The women can leave to cook meals for their families, to take a child to school or out to play. Preschool children go with their mothers to sweatshops and play beside the sewing machines. "It's not an ideal situation," one mother said to me, "but the children must be cared for and the family must eat."

There have been cases of outrageous exploitation. But, as one informant told me, both employers and employees play second fiddle to larger shops downtown, from which they receive their orders, and have to be happy with the prices they can get.

In the past people seeking help would turn to the Chinese Consolidated Benevolent Association, better known as the "Six Companies" because it was formed from six earlier organizations representing many different districts in China. Formed in the

---

57 *hover* (v.) /ˋhovə(r)/: linger close by 59 *graze* (v.): touch or scrape lightly in passing 71 *ad* (n.): AE for advertisement (= Zeitungsanzeige, Inserat) 73 *sweatshop* (n.): AE shop where employees work long hours at low wages under poor working conditions 78 *preschool* (adj.): designating a child between infancy and school age, usu. between the ages of two and five (or six) 82 *outrageous* (adj.) /ɑʊtˋreɪdʒəs/: shocking; very shameless 82 **exploitation** (n.): making unethical use of for one's own profit; Ausbeutung 83 *employer* (n.): person who gives work to others 83 *employee* (n.) /ˈemplɔɪˋi/: person who works for wages 83 *play second fiddle* (to): take a less important part (than) 85 *consolidate* (v.): unite 85 *benevolent* (adj.) /bɪˋnevələnt/: kind and helpful.

1860's, it settled disputes among Chinese, who believed that prejudice against them precluded justice in the civil courts, and became a powerful economic and political force, especially in Chinatown.

"The Six Companies was the Supreme Court of the Chinese in America," said Fred Huie, a San Francisco stockbroker and former Six Companies president. "It spoke for all the Chinese in California and fought anti-Chinese legislation in America. Later it started a school to teach the children Chinese history, language, and philosophy. It helped the community build a hospital. In those days, we were not welcome in other hospitals."

Dream of America Comes True

Mr. Huie and I talked in his office in a downtown skyscraper. Education, he told me, is the key to the door leading out of the ghetto. "The Chinese have always stressed education, even if it meant depriving themselves to keep their children in school. People can overcome almost anything with education. We learned that lesson in America long ago."

Now, he noted, there are Chinese property owners in every district of the city. Chinese are found in most professions; the postmaster and a former city supervisor are Chinese.

"Today there are millionaires among San Francisco's Chinese," Mr. Huie said. "Why? Because we're thrifty, industrious, patient. There's no limit to what a Chinese can be."

Almost all affluent Chinese now live outside Chinatown. Some who remain say that the Six Companies is losing its influence; that it doesn't care about contemporary problems or finds them too large to handle.

Many conditions have improved since the turn of the century. The opium dens are gone, and there is less prostitution. The clicking sound of mah-jongg games can still be heard along the dark alleys, but large-scale gambling has decreased. The tuberculosis rate, while still high, has dropped with the availability of treatment and some public housing. But progress comes slowly in Chinatown, and patience, in the minds of the young at least, is not a popular virtue.

"The kids today," says Mr. Huie, "don't realize how long it took, and what we had to go through to reach this point."

Chinatown was once noted for having almost no juvenile delinquency. But for more than half a century, there just weren't many children in the community.
Now, many new immigrants arrive in large families. They live in crowded rooms, often with no one to look after the children, whose playgrounds are mostly streets and alleys. Chinatown has a youth problem. Street gangs with members as young as 12

---

88 *prejudice* (n.) /ˋpredʒədɪs/: opinion, like or dislike, formed before one has adequate knowledge or experience 89 **preclude** (v.) /prɪˋklud/: make impossible 92 *stock-broker* (n.): Börsenmakler 98 **downtown** (adj.): AE relating to the lower part or main business section of a city or town 98 *skyscraper* (n.): Wolkenkratzer 99 *stress* (v.): emphasize as being important 100 *deprive* (v.): keep from having, using, or enjoying 103 *property* (n.): real estate (= land, including the buildings on it) 123 *playground* (n.): place for outdoor games 124 **gang** (n.): group of persons going about together, esp. for criminal purposes.

Graffiti inside a Chinese-American housing project in San Francisco

have become heavily involved in crime, and in open warfare among themselves, more than 35 young people have died by such violence since 1973.

I met with a gang leader who had survived the street wars. We talked outside San Francisco; he has enemies in Chinatown.

Now in his 20's he had come to Chinatown from Hong Kong a dozen years ago. "When I arrived," he said, "Chinatown looked like a back alley of Hong Kong.

"I wanted to go to school. And I tried. But it didn't work. You know what happens; the other Chinese kids say they are not Chinese but Americans. They spit on me."

He dropped out of school. By 1967 he and a group of other foreign-born boys were living off what they could steal and engaging in knife fights with their American-born rivals.

Broken Promises Lead to Bloodshed

The next year many Chinatown youths met with city and community leaders to plead for help in finding employment.

"It didn't work. There were a lot of promises, but nothing changed," he said. "That was the last chance to avoid what we have today. Probably nine out of ten guys would have gone straight if the community had tried to help them. I went back to burglaries."

---

125 *warfare* (n.): fighting 127 **survive** (v.): remain alive after 136 *bloodshed* (n.): killing or wounding of people 140 *guy* (n.): AE coll. man or boy 141 *go straight*: live an honest life 141 *burglary* (n.): crime of breaking into a house by night to steal.

"The foreign-born gang grew large. Many members took jobs as bouncers and lookouts in gambling establishments (mah-jongg and fan-tan are traditional games of chance in Chinatown) in return for free meals, bail money, and legal fees. Some youths who didn't take these jobs were beaten. The gang split, and a violent battle broke out.

Street violence moved from knives to guns, and a tragic code of honor dictated that one death must be answered with another, even if the avenger didn't know the victim.

I asked the gang leader if he was afraid.

"I worry about the young ones, the 15- and 16-year-olds who want to be heroes. If I see a young one in a bar, I keep my eyes on him because I know he shouldn't be there."

We parted, going in different directions. In my jacket pocket I found a ribbon of paper, my fortune-cookie message from the evening's dinner. It said, "You have at your command the wisdom of the ages." I wonder.

---

142 *bouncer* (n.): AE sl. man hired to remove very disorderly people from a nightclub, restaurant, etc.; Rausschmeißer 143 *lookout* (n.): Aufseher in einer Spielhalle 143 *establishment* (n.): business; house 144 *bail money* (n.): money deposited with the court to get an arrested person temporarily released on the assurance that he will appear for trial, etc. at the proper time 147 **violence** (n.): physical force used so as to injure; violent act or deed 147 *code* (n.): system of rules and principles that has been accepted by a group of people 147 *dictate* (v.) /ˈdɪktəɪt/: vorschreiben 148 *avenger* (n.) /əˈvendʒə(r)/: person who takes vengeance (= Rache) 155 *fortune-cookie* (n.): AE a hollow Chinese cookie (small, sweet cake) with a slip of paper inside bearing a message, often one predicting the future.

*

Active Vocabulary

The numbers refer to the respective text and line: e.g. "12/117" = "text 12/line 117." References with "title" are to the title of a text: e.g. "title 6" = "title of text 6." References with "In" are to the introduction to a text: e.g. "In 4/7 " = "Introduction to text 4/line 7." References with "Con" are to the context to a text: e.g. "Con 8/2" = "Context to text 8/line 2."

aesthetic (adj.): 9/36
access (n.): 7/101
accumulate (v.): 2/73–74; 22/120
accumulation (n.): 12/2
5 **achieve** (v.): 25/26
act (n.): 22/1
adjustment (n.): 12/56
admission (n.): 22/90
advocate (v.): title 7; Con 8/1
10 **alien** (adj.): 12/20; 15/21; 22/32; title 24
alien (n.): 6/21; 25/11
allegiance (n.): 7/102; 15/11
allowance (n.): 5/73
allowance (n.): 5/78
15 **allurement** (n.): 2/98–99
amalgamate (v.): 7/104
amendment (n.): 22/32
ample (adj.): 2/73
ancestor (n.): 15/44; 16/4
20 **ancestral** (adj.): 9/24
ancestry (n.): 13/87; 22/122
anxiety (n.): 12/52
apology (n.): 4/41
apply (v.): title 4; 25/21
25 **appoint** (v.): 23/68
appropriate (adj.): 9/43; 22/12
approximately (adv.): 22/115
aspire (v.): 7/91
aspiration (n.): 7/135
30 **assimilation** (n.): title 7
asylum (n.): 2/61

basic (adj.): 6/4
board (v.): 12/26
bore (v.): 20/13
35 **bother** (v.): 23/144
but (adv.): 2/33
butt (n.): 10/70
cancel (v.): 21/212
cargo (n.): 5/54
40 **casual** (adj.): 23/110
cease (v.): 15/27
certificate (n.): 14/28
christen (v.): 1/8; 4/14
citizenship (n.): 25/1
45 **clash** (n.): 22/89
cleanse (v.): 5/34
collide (v.): 12/19
commemorate (v.): In 3/4
commitment (n.): 12/8
50 **commonplace** (adj.): 12/131
concept (n.): 13/64; 22/28
concern (n.): In 12/2
condition (v.): 12/15
confer (V.): 2/74; In 15/2
55 **congregation** (n.): 2/34; 20/10
conspicuous (adj.): 2/51
constitution (n.): 11/16
contagious (adj): 5/113
contain (v.): 2/43
60 **contemporary** (adj.): In 1/3
contradict (v.): 5/86
contribution (n.): 11/19; 13/13
cope (v.): 12/58
corpse (n.): 5/97; 23/149
65 **counterpart** (n.): 13/57
criterion (n.): 2/56
crucible (n.): title 8
crude (adj.): 10/82
curtail (v.): 6/69

70 **decade** (n.): In 2/7; 13/74; In 14/6; 22/101; 25/10

Appendix: Supplementary Material

(including developments up to 1982)
selected by the author with the aid of Manfred Strack, M.A., USIS Cultural Affairs Specialist, Düsseldorf Branch.

1: ILLEGAL ALIENS: Invasion out of Control?

(From: *U.S. News & World Report,* January 29, 1979)

Unauthorized immigrants are pouring into the U.S. by the thousands, seeking work they can't find back home. Now, Mexican oil is adding fresh complications – and hope – to efforts to cope with a nearly insoluble problem.

The guardians of America's borders, handcuffed by policy disputes at home and diplomatic hazards abroad, are falling steadily behind in their struggle to close the door to thousands of illegal aliens sneaking into the U.S. every day.

Federal officials frankly admit that they are running out of acceptable options to stem a mounting flow of unregistered immigrants estimated to have reached 800,000 a year. New arrivals add daily to an existing population of noncitizens so shadowy that its numbers are pegged anywhere from 3 million to 12 million persons.

Nearly every move dealing with those whom the government calls "undocumented workers" triggers protests from ethnic and church groups, civil-rights organizations, taxpayer lobbies, labor unions, business spokesmen and others. The issue is so emotional that even cabinet-level officials cannot agree whether illegal aliens constitute an asset or a liability to the nation. Some experts go so far as to warn that solving the problem actually could make things worse by upsetting the balance in the country's labor force.

A new complication: Mexico, believed to be the source of some 60 percent of illegal entrants to the U.S. and long shrugged off as a poverty-stricken neighbor, suddenly shows promise of supplying 30 percent of crucial U.S. oil imports by the mid-1980s. The oil, all the more attractive because it is far from the turbulence of the Middle East, could deter any U.S. efforts to get tough on illegal aliens.

For all those reasons, the immigrant issue is certain to rank high on the agenda at a meeting in Mexico City February 14–16 between President Carter and Mexican President José López Portillo.

While authorities stew over remedies, illegal entrants from Mexico and a variety of Caribbean and Latin American nations are pouring across the nation's 1,946-mile southern border – scrambling over fences, wading the Rio Grande, hiking through the desert to get into the U.S., where even menial jobs pay 10 times what the illegal immigrants could earn back home. Says Dale Cozart, agent in charge of the El Paso, Tex., Border Patrol Station: "It's like trying to push the ocean back."

The problems in halting the influx of unauthorized immigrants are compounded by complaints within the Immigration and Naturalization Service that Commissioner Leonel J. Castillo, a Mexican American, is soft on enforcement.

Meanwhile, frustration builds, prompting proposals such as that from Representative James H. Scheuer (D,N.Y.), chairman of the House Select Committee on Population, for "a firm, hard sealing of the border." Scheuer's suggestion was widely criticized, as were U.S. plans to replace 27 miles of fence along the Mexican border. Even former President Nixon, on a recent outing in Tijuana, urged Congress to allow Mexicans "to get across the border, to work with dignity and send money back home."

"Give Me Your Tired, Your Poor"

Forty-eight million immigrants have journeyed to the U.S. since 1820, to face receptions ranging from open arms and immediate work to poverty and lynch mobs. "Americans are proud of presenting the nation-of-immigrants image," notes a White House report. "In fact, behavior toward newcomers from strange lands bringing different ways has been anything but benevolent."

The invitation expressed in the Emma Lazarus poem engraved beneath the Statue of Liberty to "Give me your tired, your poor, your huddled masses yearning to breathe free" has slowly faded.

The fear of foreign-born radicals and domestic economic upheavals contributed to the decision by Congress in the 1920s to clamp restrictions on immigration. It marked the end of a two-decade period in which 14.5 million newcomers flocked to the U.S. In 1920 and 1921, some 100,000 persons of Mexican extraction chose repatriation to Mexico to escape a wave of vigilante violence in the Southwest.

Today, about 400,000 immigrants are admitted legally each year. Border patrols, prosecution of smugglers and workplace raids are used to deter illegal entrants. More than 1 million apprehensions were recorded in 1978.

Yet enforcement actions are widely regarded as stopgap measures until the poor countries cap their soaring birth rates and develop economies capable of absorbing their unemployed. There is little sign of those steps being taken yet. Populations of the nations supplying most of the illegal immigrants – including Mexico, Central and South America, the Philippines and Korea – are projected to jump 70 percent to 1.7 billion by the year 2000.

"I think you can slow illegal immigration, and you can regulate it and you can manage it a lot better," says Commissioner Castillo, "but I don't think you can stop it."

2: Census Finds Chinese Surpassing Japanese as Nation's Largest Asian Group

By JOHN HERBERS

The number of Chinese in the United States has grown so rapidly in recent years that they now total more than 800,000 and have surpassed the Japanese as the leading population of Asians in this country, according to 1980 census figures announced yesterday.

The rapid increase in Chinese and in people from Japan, Korea, the Philippines, India and Vietnam reflects a surge of immigration in the first decade after the lifting of restrictive quotas on Asians in the late 1960's.

The people from those six countries make up the majority of the Asian population in the United States. They have almost doubled since 1970 and now total more than three million, as measured by the 1980 census.

The Immigration and Naturalization Service confirms the growth. It reported that 1.5 million Asians were legally admitted in the 10 years ended Sept. 30, 1980.

In the decade the number of Chinese increased 85 percent for a 1980 total of 806,000, according to the Bureau of the Census.

A decade earlier, Japanese were the predominant Asians in America, with 591,000. They grew 19 percent in the decade, to 701,000 in 1980, but were surpassed not only by Chinese but by Filipinos. The Filipinos increased their numbers 126 percent, for a 1980 population of 775,000.

Koreans showed the most phenomenal growth, increasing from 69,000 in 1970 to 355,000 in 1980, a growth rate of 413 percent.

Population Gains By Asians in U.S.

	1980	1970	Percent Increase
Chinese	806,027	435,062	85.3
Filipino	774,640	343,060	125.8
Japanese	700,747	591,290	18.5
Korean	354,529	69,130	412.8
Hawaiian	167,253	100,179	67.0

Source: U.S. Census Bureau

Asian Indians numbered 362,000 and Vietnamese 262,000 in 1980. Neither had ever been counted before by the Census Bureau. But immigration officials said the vast majorities of both had come to the United States in recent years. Most of the Vietnamese were refugees who came in under immigration quotas eased especially for those displaced by the Vietnam War and other disruptions in Southeast Asia.

The increases were made more dramatic by the moderate increase shown by the United States population as a whole in the 1970's: 11.4 percent. The Census Bureau announced earlier that according to the count in April 1980, Asians and Pacific islanders who designated their nation of origin numbered 3.5 million, or 1.5 percent of the population.

Some Groups Not on List

This, however, did not include Asians from certain countries, including Thailand, Laos, Indonesia and Pakistan. Question 4 of the census form asked residents to classify themselves as one of 14 designated groups or to check "other" and write what classification they placed themselves in. These were the preliminary results:

White	188,341,000
Black	26,488,000
American Indian	1,362,000
Eskimo	42,000
Aleutian Islander	14,177
Chinese	806,000
Filipino	775,000
Japanese	701,000
Asian Indian	362,000
Korean	355,000
Vietnamese	262,000
Hawaiian	167,000
Samoan	42,000
Guamanian	32,000
Other	6,737,000

Improved Methods a Factor

The bureau is to present a breakdown later on those in the "other" category. But it is estimated that 40 percent of those who listed themselves in that category were Hispanic Americans who consider themselves neither black nor white but as belonging to a nationality not included on the census form. Many in the "other" column were Asians from various countries.

Some of the increase in the major groups was attributed to improved methods of counting by the Census Bureau, but the census report said most of the increase was due to "a high-level immigration."

For 40 years Asians and Africans were virtually excluded from entering this country by numerical limitations first prescribed by the Quota Act of 1924, which allocated entry on the basis of the national origin of the white population.

Enactment of that law followed expression of fears by some white Americans of being overrun by hordes of people of a different color, religion and customs. It was repealed in 1965 and discriminatory quotas ended by 1968.

Current laws permit the entry of 270,000 persons a year, with each nation limited to 20,000. Exceptions have been made, however, for refugee groups such as those from Southeast Asia and Cuba, and the quotas do not include relatives of immigrants who have come into the country legally. Also, there has been a large increase in recent years in the number of illegal immigrants.

The result is that a much larger percentage of the population is now of Asian, Latin American or African extraction, even though the Census Bureau's changes in classifications between 1970 and 1980 prevent precise comparisons. Some persons who listed themselves as Mexican or Puerto Rican, for example, were listed by the bureau in 1970 as white.

Bureau officials said a large increase of American Indians, to 1,362,000 from 560,000 in 1970, was a result not only of high birth rates among Indians but especially of improvements in census procedures in counting people on reservations. The heaviest concentrations of American Indians were in California, Oklahoma, Arizona, New Mexico and North Carolina.

Asians have tended to concentrate largely in the West, with California having the largest number by far of Chinese, Japanese, Filipinos, Koreans and Vietnamese surpassing any other state.

3: Education: The Bilingual Battle

(From: *U.S. News & World Report,* August 24, 1981)

The strides being made in business are not as yet being duplicated in school systems, where Hispanic children are often the victims of discrimination and neglect. Troubles range from a dropout rate as high as 85 percent in some cities to achievement scores that are two grade levels or more below national averages.

The sheer numbers of Latins flowing into the nation are overwhelming many urban school districts. They make up 30 percent of the school population in New York, Denver and Miami, 35 percent in Hartford, 45 percent in Los Angeles and 52 percent in San Antonio. School officials struggling to accommodate a flood of Hispanic children admit they have been unable to provide a quality education to the newcomers. "Most Latinos, even after 12 years in public schools, still have serious difficulties with language and other basic skills," says Lavona Zuckerman, a member of the Miami, Fla., Citizens Education Advisory Committee.

Younger Hispanic adults, however, show significant improvement over their elders. About 57 percent of Latin Americans 25 to 29 years old have completed four or more years of high school, whereas only 34 percent of Latins ages 45 to 64

Profile of Nation's 15 Million Hispanics

In the past 10 years, the number of Hispanic Americans has grown from 9.1 million to 14.6 million—a jump from 4.5 to 5.6 percent of the U.S. population. Most live in Western states and big metropolitan areas, particularly Los Angeles, New York City and Miami. For a profile of these people—

Regions: A Southwest Slant

	1970	Latest
Northeast	21%	18%
Midwest	12%	9%
South	30%	30%
West	37%	43%

States with the largest Hispanic populations are California (4,500,000), Texas (3,000,000), New York (1,700,000) and Florida (858,000).

Income: Trailing Other Groups

Median Weekly Earnings of Full-Time Workers

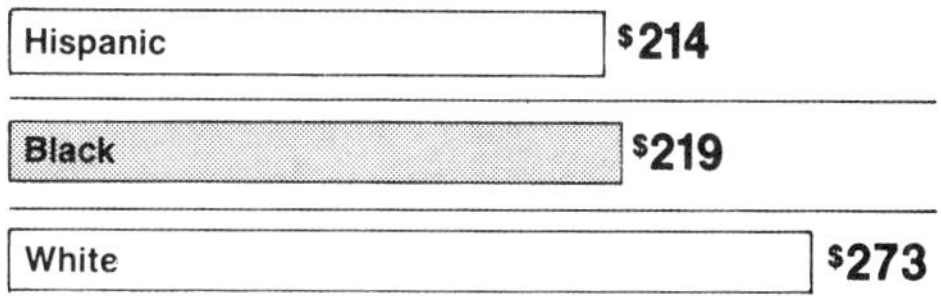

Twenty-two percent of Hispanics remain below the poverty level, compared with 27 percent for blacks and 8 percent for whites.

Origins: Mostly Mexican

Where Hispanics in U.S. Come From

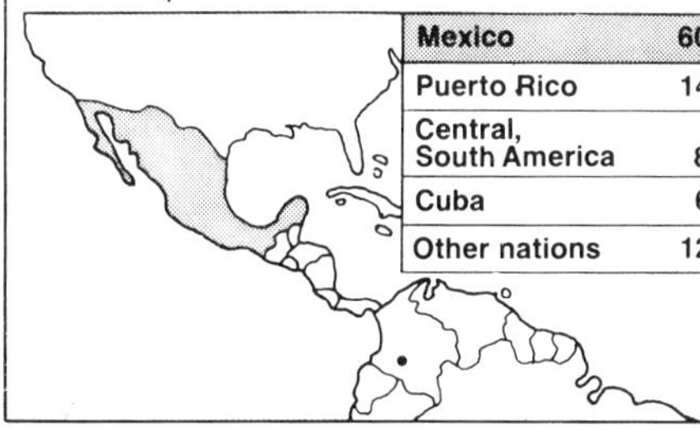

Mexico	60%
Puerto Rico	14%
Central, South America	8%
Cuba	6%
Other nations	12%

Education: Lagging Behind

Percentage Completing High School (age 25 years and over)

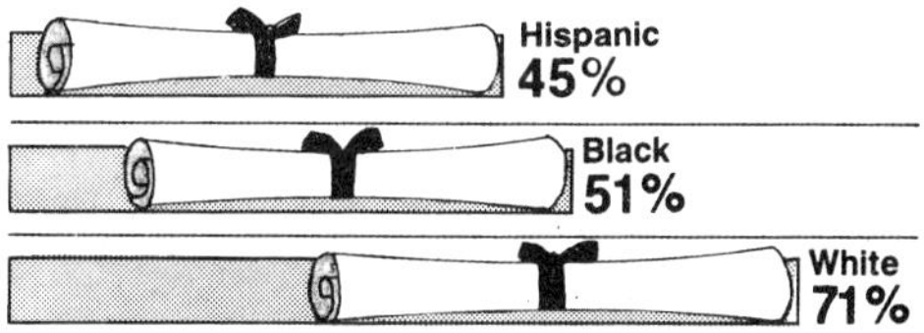

Hispanics receive less than 2 percent of all college degrees.

Note: Figures are for 1980. *USN&WR* charts—Basic data: U.S. Depts. of Commerce, Labor and Education

have done so. The percentage of Hispanics ages 25 and over with college educations also has increased from 4.8 percent in 1973 to 9 percent in 1980. Says José Longoria, an education official with LULAC: "In the 1960s, college was an end in itself for Hispanic college students. Today, they recognize the relationship between education and quality of life."

In the past, schools often contributed to the obstacles facing Hispanic students. A report issued last year by the Carnegie Corporation said schools discriminate against Hispanics by shunting them into educational tracks designed for low achievers, by classifying them as mentally retarded, by denigrating their heritage and by giving them the message that they are not expected to succeed.

Most Hispanic leaders say the only way to reverse this poor academic showing is through bilingual education, in which students are schooled in their native tongues while their proficiency in English increases. Last year, in response to a 1974 Supreme Court decision, the Department of Education issued regulations requiring schools to provide instruction in such subjects as mathematics, social studies and science in the native language of English-deficient students. The regulations sparked immediate controversy, with local schools complaining that the government was dictating the classroom curriculum. In February, Education Secretary Terrel H. Bell withdrew the rules. Bell also removed bilingual education from the administration's proposed block-grant scheme, which allows the government to continue bilingual funds to those districts that need them.

Even so, bilingual education is flourishing. As recently as 1971, no state required bilingual instruction. Now, 12 states mandate such a program and some 20 others permit it. The government provides 167 million dollars a year for instruction; states chip in 75 million. Much of the money is spent to ease an acute shortage of qualified bilingual teachers.

Yet bilingualism remains a sensitive issue, and many Americans – particularly European immigrants – favor an English-only policy as the best way to assimilate newcomers into the U.S. mainstream. This sentiment prompted signs that appeared recently in school corridors in Texas reading "Speak English – This Is America!"

4: Congress Debates Illegal Immigration

(From: *Time Magazine,* February 22, 1982)

Once inside the U.S., illegal immigrants have no lack of hiding places, and legal ones can find comfortable islands of support in proudly ethnic enclaves that have sprung up in metropolitan areas across the U.S., often giving a new vibrance to old neighborhoods. New York City is a veritable U.N. of vestpocket communities: Greeks and South Koreans in Queens, "Little Dominica" in The Bronx, "Little Jamaica" in Brooklyn. One group of prospective immigrants hopes to preserve its communal identity by gaining entrance to the U.S. They are 3,800 Assyrian and Chaldean Christians, mostly from Iraq, where authorities have tried to force them to assimilate. Now they wait in Italy, seeking refugee status in the U.S. to save their ancient ways.

The persistent diligence of those who strive to enter the U.S. has periodically prodded U.S. lawmakers to propose restrictive reforms, an idea that has gathered momentum under the Reagan Administration. One sweeping new bill that echoes the Administration's proposals for immigration reform is expected to be introduced to the Senate in the next few weeks by Republican Alan Simpson of Wyoming. Simpson, chairman of the Senate Subcommittee on Immigration and Refugee Policy, has yet to reveal the full details of his legislation, but in outline they reflect both the Administration's ideas and the conclusions based on intensive studies by his own subcommittee. Items:

ILLEGALS. The Simpson bill would attempt to legalize the status of illegal immigrants already in the country. It may reflect Administration proposals that these immigrants should apply for temporary residence status, renewable every three years. After ten years they could seek permanent residence. In the Reagan program, they would not be eligible for food stamps or welfare, or even to bring in wives and children, until the ten-year period was completed. Simpson believes that such a separation of families is too long.

INS. The Administration specifically wants to beef up surveillance in Florida and Texas to fend off new waves of Cubans, Haitians, Mexicans and others from the Caribbean and Central America. The finances are beyond the range of Simpson's bill, but he intends to press for budget increases in other legislation.

SANCTIONS. The Reagan Administration wants to impose penalties on employers of four or more people who hire illegals; Simpson would like to penalize anyone who hires a single illegal. Employers would be expected to check for proper identification: in the White House plan, a combination of such existing I.D. documents as driver's licenses, Social Security cards and selective service cards. Simpson's proposal is more controversial: a counterfeit-proof worker authorization card to be checked by employers.

QUOTAS. Simpson would impose a ceiling of about 400,000, less than half of the estimated total 1980 inflow of 880,000. It would include all immediate family members now exempt from quotas, and all refugees. The bill would restrict any country except Canada and Mexico to 20,000 immigrants. The two neighbors would be allowed 40,000 each. In line with an Administration suggestion, Simpson's bill would simply eliminate the fifth preference category for citizens' adult brothers and sisters, and expand opportunities for independent immigrants who could demonstrate that they would "integrate fully into American society."

GUEST WORKERS. The Reagan Administration advocates a two-year trial for a guest worker program for Mexican nationals, admitting up to 50,000 for periods of nine to twelve months to work in certain jobs for which American labor is scarce. Simpson would allow such a plan only as a temporary expedient.

The ambitious bill would appear to have only an outside chance of approval by the present Congress. With elections next fall, the current session will be short, and legislators in any event may well want to avoid so controversial an issue before elections. Senator Kennedy, the ranking Democrat on Simpson's committee, has already indicated that he will fight the bill's low quota limits and any guest worker program.

Yet some kind of legislation is clearly needed to sort out the inadequacies and inequities of present immigration law and deal with the unsolved issue of the illegals. If it does not happen in this Congress, it will fall to the next, or to the one after that. The problem is growing. It will not go away.

Papers for Sale

"You can get just about anything on the street as long as you can pay for it," says Omer G. Sewell, deputy director of the Los Angeles district of the U.S. Immigration and Naturalization Service. "There's a ready market for documents."

The documents to which Sewell refers are the forged papers that provide an illegal alien with bogus proof of legal status. The problem for the buyer is less the cost than the risk of being denied legal status forever. A sampling of current charges:

Green Cards. From $50 to $1,000, depending on the skill of the forger.

Social Security Cards. From $20 in Los Angeles to $500 in New York City. The cheaper cards in Los Angeles often originate in Mexico.

Birth Certificates. Easy to obtain in California for under $20. In New York City they cost up to $1,000.

Passports. A U.S. passport costs $1,000; a foreign passport runs $250, but $1,000 if it is stamped with a U.S. visa.

5: ALLAN L. DAMON: The Facts behind the Current Controversy over Immigration

(From: *American Heritage,* vol. 33, no. 1, December, 1981)

This was no ordinary fishing run for the fifty small boats that entered the Florida Strait from Key West on a late April morning last year. Their course was south by southwest to Mariel, 110 miles distant on the northern coast of Cuba. Their mission: to rescue an unknown number of political refugees who had unexpectedly been granted exit visas by Fidel Castro.

In the weeks that followed, the fifty-boat squadron was joined by hundreds of other vessels of every size and condition, their passage financed by public funds and by members of the Cuban community in Miami. For more than five months the "freedom flotilla" plied the Caribbean, bearing its human cargo to the American mainland. By the end of September, when Castro barred further emigration, 125,000 exiles had reached reception centers in Florida, Arkansas, and Pennsylvania.

At the same time, another exodus had taken place from Haiti, the poorest country in the Western Hemisphere and one of the poorest on earth. Between January and late August of 1980, more than 14,000 refugees had crossed the Caribbean to Florida in open, wooden boats, many of them dangerously overloaded and underprovisioned. One small craft, carrying a hundred passengers, had drifted for two weeks in the broiling sun before it was located and towed to safety by a Coast Guard cutter. Like the Cubans, the Haitians spoke bitterly of the hardship and oppression they had left behind. America, they said, offered them freedom and opportunity unavailable elsewhere; they were willing to risk everything for the new life the nation might provide.

The admission of such refugees has been replicated over and over again through our history: in 1975 when 120,000 Vietnamese were flown here in the two weeks that followed Saigon's fall; in the "freedom flights" which brought upward of 300,000 Cubans to Florida between 1965 and 1970; in 1956 when 21,000 Hungarians were airlifted to New Jersey in the aftermath of their abortive uprising; indeed, as long ago as 1793 when nearly 20,000 French exiles from revolution in Santo Domingo sought refuge in Pennsylvania. (The exiles were so destitute that the Pennsylvania Assembly authorized a public subscription on their behalf; Congress voted $15,000 for the cause.) As Thomas Paine had written in *Common Sense*, it was America's unique destiny to "receive the fugitive, and prepare in time an asylum for mankind."

That willingness to welcome the stranger, to offer sanctuary to the oppressed, is firmly based on the democratic ideology of the American Revolution, but it represents as well a pragmatic recognition of the central fact in our existence as a people: since the first Indians crossed the Bering Strait thousands of years ago, the American population has consisted solely of immigrants and their descendants. Immigrants from some 106 distinct ethnic groups – no one of which constitutes more than one-seventh of the whole – have transformed our land, shaped our institutions, defined our principles, and formed – in the words of Charles Andrews – "a polychrome, polyglot community" without parallel in history.

By the last quarter of the nineteenth century, the volume of immigration threatened to overwhelm the states, and, responding to demands for increased federal participation, Congress passed a comprehensive law in 1882 that opened the way to a complete federal take-over. Within a decade, the government had created a permanent Immigration Service with broad powers to set health standards, to manage immigration law, and to arrange deportation proceedings for any aliens who failed to meet the required criteria for entry. In 1892 Ellis Island was opened on the site of an old naval arsenal as the principal reception center.

Beginning with the 1882 law, the government gradually developed a policy of restricted immigration. For the first time, Congress established strict standards of admissibility. As we have seen, Chinese immigrants were barred outright; so were convicts, "lunatics," and persons likely to become public charges. In 1891 the list was extended to include polygamists, persons with "loathsome or contagious diseases," and contract laborers. Twelve years later anarchists and prostitutes were denied entry. In 1907 the Japanese, like the Chinese, were barred simply because of their race. In 1917 Congress required a literacy test for every immigrant. Any person over sixteen who could not read at least thirty words in English or some other language was to be sent home. By the end of World War I immigration law defined nearly one hundred separate conditions that might make an alien excludable.

In vetoing an earlier literacy bill in 1915, Woodrow Wilson wrote that the nation had, in the past, "generously kept our doors open to all," excepting those who were clearly unfit by reason of disease or criminal record or the like. Now, he said, Congress was proposing "to turn away from tests of character and of quality and impose tests which exclude and restrict." Was this, he asked, "the conscious ... desire of the American people?"

Within six years he had his answer. In 1921 Congress passed the first of the quota laws, which would dominate immigration policy for the next generation – all designed to reduce the immigrant flow from Southern and Eastern Europe and to prohibit entirely immigration from Asia. The last of these, the 1952 McCarran-Walter Act, passed over the veto of President Truman, added a provision empowering the Immigration Service to screen all applicants for signs of "subversive behavior."

Current policy is contained in the Hart-Celler Act of 1965. There already had been erosion of the quota system through various postwar measures allowing the entry of certain national groups, as in the Displaced Persons directives signed by President Truman in successive years from 1945 to 1952. Moreover, the role America had assumed as "leader of the free world" stood in sharp contrast to the exclusionary policies embodied in immigration law.

The Hart-Celler Act retained an annual quota as necessary to orderly growth but removed the artificial – and often biased – criteria of past admissions practices in favor of broadly based standards that gave all nationalities equal access on a first-come, first-served basis. Extra-quota status was extended to certain classes of immigrants (among them, immediate relatives of naturalized citizens and persons with special technical skills). Other reforms made it easier for the President to admit refugees, as in the Cuban exodus in 1981.

Now more than a decade old, the Hart-Celler Act has changed the face of the immigrant population, three-fourths of whom in recent years have been Asiatics or Latin Americans. Its liberalized provisions for nonquota entry have led to a steady increase in the number of aliens seeking permanent residence and of refugees requesting asylum. From 1978 to 1980 nearly 2,000,000 legal immigrants entered the country, pushing the immigration rate above 2.8 per thousand U.S. population for the first time in half a century. In addition, upward of 1,000,000 aliens illegally crossed the nation's borders. Responding to public alarm over that sudden surge of immigrants, President Reagan and some members of Congress argued that existing policies were out of control and that the Hart-Celler Act needed revision.

In mid-March, 1981, Senator Walter D. Huddleston of Kentucky introduced a comprehensive reform bill that would limit total immigration to 350,000 aliens a year, eliminate all special-status admissions above that ceiling, and restrict the entry of refugees by forcing the President to admit them under the annual quota or to borrow against future quotas. The Huddleston bill, jointly sponsored by eight other senators, also called for civil and criminal penalties for employers who hire illegal aliens and proposed tripling the size of the Border Patrol to 6,000 officers.

By midsummer, the Reagan administration offered further legislation to deal with illegal border-crossers. Arguing that "no free and prosperous nation can by itself accommodate all those who seek a better life," Mr. Reagan asked Congress to consider three specific measures: a law to prohibit the hiring of illegal aliens (punishable by a civil fine of up to $1,000 for each person so hired); the granting of legal status to the several million illegal aliens already residing here (provided they had entered the United States before January 1, 1980); and the creation of a "guest worker" program whereby 100,000 Mexicans would be admitted over two years to take jobs for which domestic labor was unavailable or in short supply.

As in earlier periods of high unemployment and economic distress, the lines are again drawn between those who argue for sharply reduced quotas and those who invoke the past as evidence that the nation must continue to accept responsibility for the oppressed from other lands. And once again Congress and the President must strike a delicate balance between them.